As man has
within him
a pool of blood,
wherein the lungs
as he breathes
expand and
contract,
so the earth has
its ocean,
which rises and
falls every six
hours with the
breathing of the
world.

Leonardo da Vinci
(1452-1519)

United States, Hawaii

Namibia. Ruacana Falls

BY MAGGIE BLACK

Water, life force

About the author

Maggie Black is an independent writer and
editor on social issues relating to international
development, particularly in the fields of children's
and women's rights, and water. She has written
three historical studies of social development ideas
as reflected in the evolution of major international
organisations, including: Children first: The story of
UNICEF (OUP and UNICEF, 1996), and A cause for
our times: OXFAM, the first 50 years (OUP and
OXFAM, 1992). She has also written a number of
other shorter books and publications, including:
AIDS and Asia: A Development Crisis (UNDP, 1992),
Women and children: A development priority
(UNICEF, 1993); In the twilight zone: Child
workers in the hotel, tourism and catering industry
(ILO, 1995); Child domestic workers: A handbook
for researchers (Anti-Slavery International and
IPEC/ILO, 1997); Children in conflict: a child rights
emergency (UNICEF UK, 1998); Learning what
works: A 20 Year Retrospective View on
International Water and Sanitation Cooperation
(World Bank/UNDP, 1998); Early Marriage: Child
Spouses (ICRC/UNICEF, 2001), and The No-
Nonsense Guide to International Development
(Verso/NI, 2002). Maggie Black is widely travelled
in the developing world, especially in East Africa
and South Asia, working as a consultant for
organisations such as UNICEF, HR Wallingford,
WaterAid, Anti-Slavery International, IPEC/ILO, SCF
and Oxfam. Between 1979 and 1987, she was Editor
of Publications for UNICEF, based in New York. She
has also been an Editor of New Internationalist
magazine, and has written for The Guardian, The
Economist and the BBC World Service.

Water, life force
First published in 2004 in the UK by
New Internationalist™ Publications Ltd
55 Rectory Road
Oxford OX4 1BW, UK
www.newint.org
New Internationalist is a registered trade mark.

Cover image: Gianni Baldizzone

Design by Barbara Willi, Zürich, Switzerland

Printed by C&C Printing Offset, Hong Kong

British Library Cataloguing-in-Publication Data.
A catalogue record for this book is available
from the British Library.

Library of Congress Cataloguing-in-Publication
Data.
A catalogue for this book is available from the
Library of Congress.

ISBN 1-904456-12-X

CONTENTS

CHAPTER 1

Elemental fluid

Dewdrop

Water was
the matrix of
the world and of
all its creatures.
All the metals,
all the stones,
all the glittering
rubies, shining
carbuncles,
crystals, gold
and silver are
derived from it.

Paracelsus, Swiss physician
and alchemist (1493-1541)

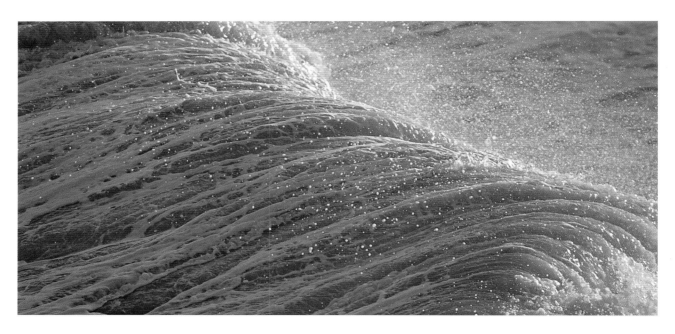

France, Normandy

A drop of water. A pearl. Which is more precious? The water of course, whose beauty the pearl tries to evoke. A pearl may be infinitely rarer, but even at its best is a pale imitation. As rain, as ice crystal, as snow-flake, as spray, the drop without which all life on earth would cease is a pearl beyond price.

A drop which fell from a rain-cloud
Was disturbed by the extent of the sea;
'Who am I in the ocean's vastness?
If IT is, then indeed I am not!'
While it saw itself with the eyes of contempt
A shell nurtured it in its bosom.
The heavens so fostered things
That it became a celebrated, a royal pearl:
Becoming high from being low
It knocked on the door of nothingness:
Until being came about.
Saadi of Shiraz, 13th C (Persia)*

*The country named in brackets is the location for the quote or extract.

Water powers our minds and bodies more elementally than any other substance. Thousands of years ago, humankind understood that without water, there will be nothing. Nothing flowing through the intricate network of veins and arteries in the earth's body, lubricating its soils, shaping its cavities and depressions, and fueling its inner store of fertility. Without water there will be nothing to quench thirst, nothing to bathe in, nothing to wash away impurities. No green shoots, no animal or insect life, no fish nor fowl, no milk, no blood, no semen. No shelter, tools or bricks; no pots, fabrics or artistic life. No mines, boats, trains, books.

Rahiman pani rakhiye.
Bin pani, sab soon.
Pani gaye na ubre,
Moti, manas, choon.
Rahim the poet says: Conserve water.
Without water, nothing is there.
If water goes,
Pearl, mankind, and lime will not survive.
Abdul Rahim Khankhana, 16th C (India)

A water molecule spends 4,000 years in the ocean, 400 years on land, and 10 days as vapor in the atmosphere.

India, Goa. Crossing a monsoon-swollen river

Bolivia, High Andes. Bus crossing a flooded plateau

10 / The total water on earth is 1.4 billion cubic km, in oceans, lakes, glaciers, rivers, streams and groundwater.

Water as creator

Greece, Rhodes
At a fountain in the old town

Since earliest times people have honored water, worshiped water, granting it a special place in their language, myths and rituals. Gods and goddesses send soothing rain to cool the earth and make it fruitful, or tempestuously thunder, flooding it in punishment.

Water nymphs sport with river gods. Mermaids and sirens summon the unwary. Narcissus stares at his reflection in the world's oldest mirror. Ix Chel, the Mayan goddess, pours torrential rains from her jug. The Inuit's deity, Nerrivik, is a goddess of water, beautiful, haughty, and rules her realm with ferocious justice. When she withholds her gifts, no-one can live.

In the Hindu pantheon, water holds a spiritual value. The Ganges is holy, and all whose ashes are dispersed in it go straight to heaven. So is the Narmada. Shiva, god of destruction, sent it forth to release the world from evil.

O copper-coloured water
Below a copper-coloured sky.
From Shiva's penance you became water.
From water you became a woman
So beautiful that gods and ascetics
Their loins hard with desire
Abandoned their contemplations
To pursue you.
Once and only once
In the turning Wheel of Existence
The Terrible One was moved to laughter.
Looking from his inward contemplation
To watch you, the Destroyer said,
Oh damsel of the beautiful hips,
Evoker of Narma, lust,
Be known as Narmada
Holiest of rivers.

Indian raga

India, Agra. Taj Mahal

Earth's annual rainfall is 110,000 cubic km, of which around 40,000 cubic km lands on the surface and becomes run-off. The rest evaporates.

Water, the element

Water was one of Aristotle's four elements, with earth, fire and air. But long after the composition of the other three had been chemically understood, water was still regarded as indivisible into constituent parts.

Not until the end of the 18th century was water finally demonstrated to be a 'mixture' of elements. Many scientists played a part in the prestige of this discovery. First comes the – very – non-conformist English minister, Joseph Priestley who experimented with oxygen. Then the reclusive and eccentric chemist, Henry Cavendish, whose enquiries into 'factitious airs' led him to hydrogen. But the chemist with the highest claim is a supremely distinguished Frenchman, Antoine Laurent Lavoisier.

In 1783, Lavoisier announced to the Academy of Sciences in Paris that water was a compound of two parts hydrogen to one of oxygen. Unfortunately his many brilliant discoveries did not save him from the guillotine. He was executed in 1794, when the president of the tribunal declared: **'La République n'a pas besoin de savants'** (The Republic has no need of intellectuals). Thus was the life of the man who gave us H_2O dismissed.

Water is capable of gluing itself together or falling into myriad parts. It blends with other things, transporting them away or becoming a solution, a new liquid altogether. Or it may be steamed away and leave other matter, solidified, behind. Water refuses to be fixed in any place or assume a permanent shape. Apparently flavorless, odorless and colorless, it disobeys all known chemical laws. At different temperatures and under different pressures, it not only changes shape and weight, but becomes different things.

Water molecules clamp on to each other with a tenacity greater than that of the molecules of some metals. The infinite string they form creates an ephemeral molecular lattice that is incessantly remodeled from one fraction of a second to another. Some liquids are nothing but disorderly solids. Water is a structured liquid of elementary constituents that spontaneously associate with one another; this results in the most singular behavior.

Water: A spectacular celebration, Hans Silvester, 2001

If all the rain and snow that fell over the course of a year was spread evenly over the earth, it would form a layer roughly 760 mm deep.

Philippines, Catanduanes province, Virac

Water in history

Yemen. Ancient reservoir in the village of Thulla

The people of the ancient world became expert at capturing water, at building structures to hold water, channel water, tame water and harness water for every human use. By the time the first cities were built, in the valleys of the Nile, Tigris, Euphrates, Indus and Huang rivers, they had already become practised hydraulic engineers. For 'civilizations' to develop, there were two pre-conditions. One was an agricultural surplus. The other was the skill to capture and channel freshwater. The latter was paramount, because the agricultural surplus also depended on it.

The oldest rock-hewn water cisterns, built to collect rainwater from roofs, from paved squares, even from water-bearing strata below ground, appeared in Palestine and Greece before 2000 BC. The first dams to retain large volumes of water were built in Jordan and Egypt even earlier, between 3000 and 2500 BC. By the middle of 100 AD, covered tanks and cisterns with huge storage volumes were being built. The Romans with their aqueducts and baths, fountains and drainage, were superb water maestri.

Somalia, Belet Uen
Water storage jars

Thus, the story of human settlement and the flowering of civilizations both ancient and modern begins with water.

Human settlements began where people saw the chance of establishing sustainable lifestyles on fertile land where water was more or less regularly available. Thus the inhabitants came to create social arrangements for the sharing of land and water within their communities.

Because it is fixed and stable, land can be divided. Thus land has the potential to become, as it has done for many societies, the foundation of private property, personal wealth and inheritance. By contrast water has to be a communal asset because it will not stay still. For thousands of years, legal systems across the world have accepted and insisted that there can be no owner-ship of common water.

Troubled Water, David Kinnersley, 1988

The hydrologic cycle

Even the ancient sages had a hydrological understanding. Hindu texts written 800-600 BC contain many observations on river courses, dikes, water reservoirs, wells and water-lifting devices. One of the **Upanishads**, or Vedic hymns, says: 'The rivers... all discharge their waters into the sea. They lead from sea to sea, the clouds raise them to the sky as vapor and release them in the form of rain.'

This is the oldest reference to what every schoolchild today is taught to call 'the hydrologic cycle'. It shows that, back in antiquity, efforts were already being made to interpret natural phenomena and explain wind and rain.

Today, we can be more precise on how the hydrologic cycle renews our global freshwater supply. The sun shining on the oceans makes seawater evaporate and turn into clouds. Under metrological influences, the moisture condenses and returns to earth as rain, hail, and snow. These precipitations are irregularly dispersed between land masses, and between mountains, coasts, and plains. Much evaporates. The rest lands as run-off and provides our renewable freshwater.

Until recently water was seen as an infinite resource which would never run dry, courtesy of modern civil engineering to move it about the landscape at will. But more traditional cultures, relying on natural resources – cultivation of rain-fed crops, forest products, livestock and fish – behave with more respect for water. Belatedly, the world is waking up to their wisdom.

O ye Waters that be above the Firmament, bless ye the Lord;
O ye Showers and Dew, bless ye the Lord;
O ye Dews and Frosts, bless ye the Lord;
O ye Ice and Snow, bless ye the Lord;
O ye Lightnings and Clouds, bless ye the Lord;
O ye Wells, bless ye the Lord;
O ye Seas and Floods, bless ye the Lord;
O ye Whales and all that move in the Waters, bless ye the Lord:
Praise him and magnify him for ever.
Benedicite, Omni Opera, The Book of Common Prayer, 1562

Clouds over Angola

The average life-span of a cloud is no more than ten minutes.

Brazil/Argentina border. Swallows at the Iguazú Falls

Turks and Caicos Islands. Storm

21 /   Oceans contain 97% of the water on earth, and cover 71% of its surface.

Water the destroyer

The drip, drip of water eats away rock. The sudden deluge of water submerges everything in its path. Where water flows as sheets, whole surface layers can be removed. All rivers erode their banks, and waves erode the shores of lakes and the sea, transforming rocks into sediments and landforms.

The vital link between the environment and water's behavior was understood in ancient times, in images which now have the capacity to haunt our far more over-crowded world. In Greece, in the 5th century BC, Plato lamented: 'What now remains at Attica compared with what then existed is like the skeleton of a sick man, all the fat and soft earth having wasted away and only the bare framework of the land being left.'

Coastal dwellers, people such as the Aztecs in Mexico who built cities around great lakes, and those living along the banks of big rivers – the Mississippi, the Rhine, the Ganges, the Zambezi and the Yangtze – have always been familiar with water's destructive power. Torrential rains and storms wash thousands of dwellings and livelihoods away. Their disastrous effects are made worse by – and contribute to – large-scale erosion.

Today, climate change is making water more temperamental. In 2000, Mozambique experienced its worst floods for 150 years, with 700 people drowned and 550,000 displaced. In 2002, two weeks' torrential rain in August filled the Danube to record heights. This and other swollen rivers caused the worst floods in Europe in 200 years, with serious damage in Prague, Dresden and many other towns.

In the UK, the storm of January 1953 was the worst peace-time disaster ever recorded. On the east coast, 307 people were killed and 30,000 evacuated. In the Netherlands, 1,835 people were drowned as dikes gave way.

It had been blowing hard and I felt disturbed, so I went with my wife to have a look at the tide coming in at 4 pm. It was a strange sight, the previous tide had not gone out, it had been penned in the Wash by the wind. It was as if we were looking uphill, the new tide was coming in on top of the old.

At 6 pm the water was rushing up from the sea. I told the wife to gather up the foster son, Christopher. The water was coming up through the floorboards. I told the American couple next door to get out quick. The girl was pregnant, and she had the baby next day, no doubt it was the shock.

Ivor Stuart, survivor (UK)

During the 1990s, weather- and water-related disasters – floods and droughts – claimed 71% of all lives lost to disasters.

Cuba, Havana. Waves on the Malecon

Surprising water

Tunisia. Sparkling water

Contrary to the virtues of sweetness and purity that prose and poetry tend to celebrate, water is an aggressive substance with many surprises at its disposal. Its purity is a myth: it is always an aqueous solution, containing some element or trace of something else. Its innocent appearance is deceptive too. As well as tumbling over waterfalls, gurgling in brooks, sparkling on lakes, and filling our spirits with wonder, it is capable of treachery.

Water, with its extraordinary power of solvency, can invisibly secrete poisonous minerals and corrosive acids, giving nothing away by taste or appearance. Water can be a great contaminator too, providing a safe habitat for predatory insects and parasites such as the malarial mosquito. It is also the perfect medium for spreading germs and agents of disease.

If water's quality is duplicitous, its physical form can also betray. The smallest crack in a water container, and it escapes clean away. In the heat of the sun, it may transpire into vapor, eluding capture. In sub-zero temperatures, it expands into ice, a hard, dangerous and brutal substance.

Yet whatever water does and however fickle it may be, it has to be treated tenderly and forgiven. The terrestrial environment, the living planetary fabric, owes everything to water. Humanity's existence depends upon it and we treat water disrespectfully – as we have begun to do today – at our peril.

Some say the world will end in fire,
Some say in ice.
From what I've tasted of desire
I hold with those who favor fire.
But if it had to perish twice,
I think I know enough of hate
To say that for destruction ice
Is also great
And would suffice.

Robert Frost (1874-1963)

Freshwater freezes, becoming ice, at 0°C (32°F); and boils, becoming steam, at 100°C (212°F).

CHAPTER 2

Water in the landscape

Morocco. Atlas Mountains

Nothing in
the world is as
soft and yielding
as water.
Yet for dissolving
the hard
and inflexible,
nothing can
surpass it.

Lao-Tze,
Chinese philosopher
(c604-c521 BC)

Morocco. Todra Gorge

Water is instrumental in sculpting the topography of the planet. It flows over and around the landforms created by the clashing of tectonic plates, carving out mountains and opening up oceans, nestling into lakes and bursting out from springs, converging from tiny streams into vast rivers that disgorge into the sea. Water's work in etching and refining the landscape – chip, chipping it away, with attention to the smallest detail – never ends. From the moment the earth's crust solidified, water has never stopped wearing it away.

Ice sheets are great hewers of the landscape. When drops of water infiltrate the pores of rocks and then freeze, the larger volume exerts an irresistible pressure, splitting them apart. As glaciers move, they scour away soil and boulders, pushing them aside to form moraines. The largest continental ice-sheet in the world covers Greenland. In the Antarctic, mountain ranges as high as the Appalacians are hiding under the flat white frozen surface.

A thousand years ago the hunter's world was made of ice and darkness, water and light. The seasons rocked back between light and dark and the ice was always moving. The land was an ocean that broke against bodies of water, shattering into islands big and small. Tides armwrestled pack ice until it accordioned up against itself, finally falling onto the mainland's shore. Glaciers calved great slabs of ice as big as convention centers and as fanciful as the Taj Mahal, and these sailed down the fjords all summer, their arches, towers, and shoulders collapsing in sudden heat as if from a fit of laughter.

This Cold Heaven, Gretel Ehrlich, 2003 (Greenland)

Antarctica. Chinstrap and gentoo penguins at rest on the ice

Only 0.007% of the earth's freshwater supply is accessible and usable for humanity's essential needs. 70% is locked up in the ice-caps.

China. Rice terraces

31 /   Of all the land under cultivation in the world, 83% is watered only by the rain and 17% by irrigation.

Lakes

Kenya, Lake Victoria
Fishing boats from Dunga
Beach set sail at dawn

When ice sheets disappear, empty bowls remain where the ice was thickest. They are then flooded either by the sea – as was the Baltic – or by freshwater – as were the Great Lakes of North America. The English Lake District was also created in this way. Where a relatively narrow glacier flows into the sea, the trough it excavates may later form a fjord, known in Scotland as a sea loch.

The lochs of Scotland, carved out long ago by ice like the fjords of Norway, are spectacular, wild, and awe-inspiring. The history they have seen, with its massacres, its bravery, its heroic blood-feuds between clans, reflects the landscape's majesty and menace. The song of Loch Lomond was written by a highlander awaiting execution after the Battle of Culloden where the 1745 rising against the English ended. The low road is the road of death, which his spirit will travel faster than his companions returning on the high road.

Oh ye'll take the high road,
An' I'll take the low road,
An' I'll be in Scotland afore ye,
But me an' my true love will never meet again
On the bonnie, bonnie banks o' Loch Lomond.

The song of Loch Lomond, Donald MacDonald of Keppoch

Norway, Spitzbergen. Icemelt due to global warming

The last ice age began around 18,000 years ago, ending 6-8,000 years later. At the outset, the sea level was about 120 meters/393 ft lower than today.

...and rivers

Rivers play a major part in molding the landscape. They cut channels and etch valleys across the earth's surface, seeking out the softer sediments in the land's formation. In places where the geological contrasts are acute, this can have extraordinary results, as at Niagara between the US and Canada, Iguazú on the Brazil-Argentina border, and the Victoria Falls.

Known locally as **Mosi oa tunya** – 'the smoke that thunders' – these are the most stupendous waterfalls in the world. They separate Zambia from Zimbabwe, and run on through five spectacular gorges gouged in a zig-zag through soft sandstone strips in between layers of hard basalt rock.

16th November, 1855: We came in sight, for the first time, of columns of vapour, appropriately called smoke, rising at a distance of five or six miles, exactly as when large tracts of grass are burning in Africa. Five columns now arose, and bending in the direction of the wind, they seemed placed against a low ridge covered with trees. The tops of the columns appeared to mingle with the clouds.
Missionary Travels and Researches in South Africa, David Livingstone (1813-1873)

Rivers also act as a means of transporting particles eroded from surface rocks from uplands to lowlands and eventually to the sea. Streams draining into larger rivers from adjacent land also contain organic matter and dissolved plant nutrients. And of course, wastes. They act as the world's inbuilt laundry and washing up system – which is today becoming seriously overloaded.

When rivers start their journey, usually as a headstream or highland brook, they are small and torrential and few aquatic animals can survive. A little lower, trout can buffet what is still a fast-flowing stream. Lower down, silt and mud collect, and plant growth begins. In the lowland reach, the water flows slowly, the river meanders, and plant and animal life is varied. In the final leg of its pilgrimage, the river flows out across the coastal plain, sometimes becoming vast – the Amazon at its mouth is over 200 miles wide – before finally reaching the sea.

Rivers are a source of plenty. They supply domestic water, irrigation, water for cooling, cleaning and industrial purposes, and for energy generation. They also provide an important source of food – fish, and are routes of transport and trade. They supply inspiration to artists, poets, priests, scientists and philosophers. This tends to happen most where rivers reign supreme, as in Egypt, Iraq, Brazil, China, Bangladesh or Vietnam.

Knowing my own quantity,
It is I, I tug, I call upon all of my roots,
the Ganges, the Mississippi,
The thick spread of the Orinoco,
the long thread of the Rhine,
The Nile with its double bladder.
Cinq grandes odes, Paul Claudel, 1913

Brazil. Dense forest on one bank, cleared farmland on the other

35 / The word 'meander' comes from a river of this name in Asia Minor, which flows in very pronounced rhythmical loops.

Australia. Tasmanian Wilderness

A stream from far-off mountains at last reached the sands of the desert. When it tried to cross this barrier, it found that its waters disappeared.

A hidden voice, coming from the desert, whispered: 'The wind crosses the desert and so can the stream'. The stream objected that it was dashing itself against the sand, and only getting absorbed. Whereas the wind could fly.

'In this way you can only become a marsh. You must allow the wind to lift you as vapour and carry you across the desert.' The stream objected. How would it regain itself at the other side?

'The wind,' said the sand, 'performs this function. When it drops you as rain, you will become again a river.' When he heard this, the stream began dimly to remember a state in which he had been held in the arms of the wind.

And the stream raised his vapour into the wind's embrace, which bore him away, letting him fall softly as soon as they reached the roof of a mountain. Then he reflected: 'Now I have learned my true identity.'

But the sands already knew this, because they had seen it all before. That is why it is said that the stream of life is written in the sands.

The Tale of the Sands, Awad Afifi (Algeria 19th C)

Watersheds and river basins

Water always flows downhill towards the river valley in a watershed or 'catchment' – the area of drainage encased by a perimeter of highland and the sea. Rain falling on a spine of hills will end up in different catchments, depending on which slope it landed. Some of it will permeate the earth and recharge aquifers – water lodes nestling in rock crevices and spongy formations underground. The rest will become run-off, joining the surface streams making up the whole river basin.

Rivers have often been used as 'natural' boundaries for nations, states, districts, and counties. Parts of the Danube, Uruguay, Jordan, Zambezi, Niger and a host of great and lesser streams have been co-opted for this purpose. But this creates anomalies. The banks of rivers have always been a magnet for human settlement, but the riverine communities that grow up along them are usually united by kin, language, and their joint dependence on the waters they share. Their artificial division into separate, competing, political entities – especially in Africa – has caused no end of grief.

In today's water-short world, it is frequently proposed that the catchment or river basin be made the basis for the management of water so that it can be equitably shared. It is, unfortunately, too late to make them the standard basis of political and administrative organization too. Increasing demand and growing tensions between upstream and downstream users of the same source are the main cause of alarm that, before long, there will be 'water wars'. There are already major disputes.

The Nile's waters are critical to Egypt which receives no usable rain and has no other water except a few rapidly depleting aquifers under the desert sands. Only 2 per cent of Egypt is not desert, and its 68 million people are entirely dependent on the river. As population rises and lifestyles change, demand is growing. The Nile, however, flows through eight other countries before reaching Egypt, and all want their share. Most of its water comes from the Blue Nile, rising in Ethiopia, which frequently points out to Egypt its dependence on Ethiopian bounty. Sudan dominates the White Nile. In the mid-1980s, Egypt was on the point of ordering air attacks against Khartoum because of perceived water threats. Up to now, poverty and civil war have inhibited major construction in either country to divert water on a large scale.

Water Wars, Marq de Villiers, 2001

Canada, Hudson's Bay. Caribou migrating across the tundra in summer

River basins can be vast: the Nile's is more than 1.3 million sq miles; that of the Congo – a shorter river – 1.4 million sq m.

Unfair water

Philippines, Manila. Child working to provide a banana-leaf umbrella

Shakespeare says that it rains equally upon the just and the unjust, pointing to its equalizing capacity. But that's only one part of the picture. Not only are those lucky enough to live on river banks, lakes, and over aquifers privileged compared to those who do not; rain is highly discriminatory too. If you spend 100 years in the middle of the Sahara, you may encounter less rainfall than on just one wet day in Hawaii.

The typical annual rainfall of western Europe and on the prairies of the US and Canada is around 800 mm. But many places, especially in sub-tropical zones, receive a lot more or a lot less. Mountainsides receive the most generous bursts of rain, especially if they are in the middle latitudes and face west, because the prevailing winds force clouds full of water to collide with them. Over the ridge on slopes in the rain shadow, half as much may fall.

The wettest place in the world is Cherrapunji, in Assam, India. In 1850, British naturalist Joseph Hooker spent the monsoon months in Cherrapunji. He was fascinated by the 'the extraordinary exuberance of species' associated with the wetness – the richest abundance in all of Asia, or so.he believed. The rainfall positively astounded him.

The first person to draw this to the attention of the world was a Mr Yule, who stated that in the month of August, 1841, 264 inches fell, or 22 feet; and that during five successive days, 30 inches fell every 24 hours. During the seven months of our stay, upwards of 500 inches fell, so the total annual fall perhaps greatly exceeded the 600 inches, or 50 feet, registered in succeeding years.

Joseph Hooker, 1850 (Cherrapunji, India)

Raindrops represent those particles of moisture within a floating cloud which have become too heavy for the air to support them any longer.

The monsoon

In temperate parts of the world, rainfall does not restrict itself to certain times of year. But in tropical areas, rainfall is more predictable, coming in a 'rainy season' around which crops are planted and harvested. Every year's dry season is an ordeal. The rains are longed for and celebrated when they arrive.

The monsoon dominates the life-cycle of most peoples in southern and eastern Asian countries such as India, Nepal, Bangladesh, Indonesia, and Vietnam. In the weeks before the rains, temperatures climb through the roof, tempers fray, anxieties become acute. Then the black monsoon clouds release their deluge, and dried-up river-beds begin to trickle, streams swell, tanks, wells, ponds and lakes fill up. Landscapes that were lunar in their aridity spring into life.

Not surprisingly, the monsoon is depicted in literature as the season of love, when plants and people all receive a new lease of life.

Well-formed and steady
Bulky bodied with a large belly
Blue-hued, with great majesty
The rain-cloud, may it rain!
May you thunder, God of Rain!
Destroy the crow's eternal thirst
And destroy his sorrow,
Relieve me of my sorrow!
By the truth of these words
May rain-clouds shower well!

A chant to invoke the rain-god, Pajjunna, from Buddhist scriptures (Sri Lanka)

Bangladesh. Walking to market through the flood

India, Mumbai. Monsoon lashing Marine Drive

43 / The southwest Indian monsoon hits the southern tip of the country on or about June 1st and travels rapidly north, accompanied by storms, winds, and floods.

Drought and desert

Drought occurs when it doesn't rain – or rains far less than is usual. A year with 500 mm (20 inches) of rain would be miraculous in parts of Mongolia or the Sahel, but a disaster for Miami, Djakarta, or Nairobi. Cities which have expanded in times of plentiful rainfall and then endure prolonged drought suffer worse than true deserts, such as the Sahara, Kalahari or Negev. These cannot really experience drought because rainlessness is their norm.

Rare is the place on earth, however arid, without some nomadic or hunting people – the Fulani of West Africa, the San of South Africa, the Bedouin of the Middle East, aboriginal people in Australia – eking out a living in the desert or at its edge. The margins on which they survive are extremely fine. They are used to laying up reserves to cope with extended periods of poor rain, but successive years of drought can bring them to their knees.

The effects of drought can be worsened by over-grazing in fragile, semi-desert areas. This happened in the Sahel on the southern edge of the Sahara, after herders were given vaccinations for their cattle, deeper wells, and encouraged to seek pasture further north. The loss of vegetation decimated the herds and many died of starvation in the 1970s and 1980s. The encroachment of the desert sands into once cultivable areas of the Sahel has since been remorseless.

Namibia, Kalahari Desert
The San people use ostrich eggs to store water

When I was a boy, the ponds and waterholes used to last the whole year through. Now they are dry and empty.

When the rains came and filled the oshanas **(streams), we used to take our baskets and go fishing. Now the fish baskets hang from the roof poles as ornaments. They are never used.**

We walked to school through long grass as high as our arm-pits, as far as you could see. Now the grass has all gone and there is nothing for the cattle to eat.

Abraham, from the Cuvelai basin (Namibia)

33% of the earth's surface is arid or semi-arid. Another 11% is covered in ice and a further 10% is tundra.

Algeria, Sahara Desert. Mirage

Australia, Northern Territory. Dead trees near Gove

Niger. Desert border in the Sahel

47 / 1,093 billion ha of land (UN estimate) has been degraded by water erosion; 43% of this is due to human and animal removal of natural vegetation.

The power of water

CHAPTER 3

Brazil, Paraná River. Itaipu hydro-electric power plant

Not a single drop of water received from rain should be allowed to escape into the sea without being utilized for human benefit.

King Prakrama Bahu
the Great of Sri Lanka
(1153-1186)

To control water is to control life and livelihoods. So there is a strong connection between power over water and power over people.

This perception became the leitmotif of the theory of history developed by Karl Wittfogel, who studied the civilizations described by Marx as 'oriental despotisms'. He suggested that early empires such as those in China, Egypt and Mesopotamia were dependent on hydraulic might.

Primitive man has known water-deficient regions since time immemorial; but while he depended on gathering, hunting and fishing, he had little need for planned water control. Only after he learned to utilize the reproductive process of plant life did he begin to appreciate the agricultural possibilities of dry areas, which contained sources of water supply other than on-the-spot rainfall – only then did the opportunity arise for despotic patterns of government and society.
Oriental Despotism, Karl August Wittfogel, 1957

Throughout history, kings, maharajahs, even Presidents, have identified themselves with monumental hydraulic works. When the 725 foot (221 meter) Hoover Dam on the Colorado river was inaugurated in 1936, it was the highest in the world and truly awe-inspiring. Herbert Hoover's engineering supremacy took him up the ladder of political power and into the White House.

President Abdel Nasser of Egypt surpassed this engineering marvel with the Aswan High Dam, begun in 1960. President Kwame Nkrumah of Ghana's grandiose ambitions included his own high dam on the Volta, the Akosombo, which created the largest reservoir in the world.

In 1993, Saddam Hussein set his engineers to drain Iraq's southern marshlands, displacing 100,000 Marsh Arabs and destroying their way of life. This was a throwback to biblical leaders such as King Nebuchadnezzar of Babylon, for whom hydraulic construction was an expression of ultimate might.

From today's and yesterday's world, the examples of rulers who combined the commandeering of water with the commandeering of people are legion. However, some such leaders have brought inestimable benefits to many of their subjects if not to all. Such a one was King Mahasena of Sri Lanka, who was deified for building a magnificent tank near his capital at Anuradhapurna in the 3rd century and solving his people's water problems.

But some self-aggrandizing schemes involving water have broken political careers too. Nkrumah's massive projects bankrupted Ghana, and he was deposed in a coup.

I made pools of water to irrigate a forest springing up with trees. Thus I gained more wealth than anyone else before me in Jerusalem.
King Solomon of Israel (1000 BC)

The Three Gorges dam in China will be the largest hydroelectric dam in the world. It will tower 575 feet/175 meters above the river and its reservoir will displace 1.9 million people.

China, Yangtze River. The Three Gorges dam will be the world's biggest

Strategic waters

Iraq. Shatt-al-Arab waterway

Water has played a vital part in the development of political terrains, countries and empires. Britain's enclosure by the sea is a classic case where watery encirclement encouraged a melting-pot of peoples within, and defense against invaders from without. These advantages were immortalized by Shakespeare well before the British Isles became a platform for colonialist expansion, or for the recovery of the continent of Europe from the grip of Hitler's tyranny.

This royal throne of kings, this scepter'd isle,
This earth of majesty, this seat of Mars,
This other Eden, demi-paradise,
This fortress built by Nature for herself
Against infection and the hand of war,
This happy breed of men, this little world,
This precious stone set in the silver sea,
Which serves it in the office of a wall.

John of Gaunt in **King Richard II**, William Shakespeare

No military commander, from Alexander the Great to General Tommy Franks, the US commander-in-chief for the second Gulf War, has neglected the role of rivers, bridges, dams and freshwater supplies in the pursuit of conquest or the strategy of defense. The story of armed campaigns throughout history and across the globe cannot be told without heroic stands on bridges or ambushes on river crossings. And cutting off a city's water supply has been a tactic of siege warfare since it was first invented.

The Incas, who undertook a rebellion in 1536 under their Emperor Manco against the Spaniards under Hernando Pizarro, were wise to the military possibilities of water. They retreated to their fortress-temple of Ollantaytambo on the Yucay river, 30 miles from Cuzco, after their greatest citadel had fallen to the Spaniards amid scenes of horror. Beseiged at Ollantaytambo, they fought valiantly against Pizarro's mounted soldiers.

Manco now released his other secret weapon. Unobserved by the Spaniards, native engineers diverted the Paracancha river along prepared channels to flood the plain. The Spanish horse-men soon found themselves trying to manoeuvre in rising water that eventually reached the horse-men's girths. The ground became so sodden that the horses could not skirmish. Pizarro realised that it was impossible to take the town and ordered a retreat.

The Conquest of the Incas, John Hemmings, 1973 (Peru)

'If you have nothing to tell us but that on the banks of the Oxus and the Jaxartes, one barbarian has been succeeded by another barbarian, in what respect do you benefit the public?' **Voltaire**, 1764

Taming the waters

Water in its fury can be so powerful that super-natural powers were traditionally called upon to control it. The experience of a storm with its wind and its deluge can be utterly terrifying, and appeared to the ancients as manifestations of God's wrath. Cyclones, typhoons and hurricanes can overpower the strongest structure, drowning people, animals and crops.

Even a heavy downpour in a tropical climate can cause havoc in homes and on the land. The driving rain eats into roofs, pours down walls, spoils, damages, drowns, flushes away seedlings, transports disease and augurs other kinds of loss.

It is drumming hard here
And I suppose everywhere
Droning with insistent ardour upon
Our roof-thatch and shed
And through sheaves split open
To lighting and rafters
I cannot make out overhead
Great water drops are dribbling
Falling like orange or mango
Fruits showered forth in the wind
In wooden bowls and earthenware
Mother is now deploying
About our roomlet and floor.

Night Rain, John Pepper Clark (Nigeria)

Given its unruly behavior, some societies have had to become adept at taming water. In China, defense against floods led to the construction of dikes along the rivers since earliest times. From the 8th century, the Yangtze was shielded from the sea for a distance of 150 miles (240 km) from its mouth by a sturdy double embankment which still stands today.

Chairman Mao Zedong was at one with earlier Chinese dictators in longing to tame the Yangtze river. He dreamed of a great bridge and a dam to reshape the river forever. The bridge he opened in 1957, naming it 'Iron and Steel Rainbow'. But the dam – the Three Gorges Dam – only began construction in 1994 after long and fierce controversy.

Strong citizen opposition forced the Chinese People's Congress to suspend plans for the dam in early 1989. But the project was almost imme-diately resurrected by Premier Li Peng, once the forces of democracy had been violently crushed in Tiananmen Square. It will control the river, its flood plains, and the future lives – for good or ill – of millions of people. The dam remains controversial: there have been human rights abuses during resettlement, technical faults, spiraling costs, and corruption scandals. Submergence in the reservoir area began in 2003.

From 1972 to 1996, floods affected 65 million people, more than any other type of disaster including war, drought and famine.

India, Mumbai. Children at play in the flooded streets

Holding back the waters

India, Narmada River. Villagers hold a ceremony below the village of Jalsindhi, soon to be flooded by a dam

It was presumed in the past that only the super-natural, through earthly intermediaries such as kings and priests, was able to exercise constraining power over water. A notorious example was the Danish-English King Canute (995-1035), who thought he could hold back the waves simply by telling the tide not to come in. Stories handed down implied that such a feat could be accomplished by faith.

And Moses stretched out his hand over the sea. And the Lord caused the sea to go back by a strong east wind all that night, and made the sea dry land, and the waters were divided.

And the children of Israel went into the midst of the sea upon the dry ground. The waters were a wall unto them on their right hand, and on their left. And the Egyptians pursued, and went in after them to the midst of the sea.

Then Moses stretched forth his hand over the sea, and the sea returned to his strength. And the Lord overthrew the Egyptians in the midst of the sea.

The waters covered the chariots, and the horse-men, and all the host of Pharaoh. There remained not so much as one of them.

The Bible, Exodus 14

Gradually, however, the role of the Almighty was replaced by that of the hydraulic engineer. Centuries of effort to contain the incursions of the North Sea made Holland the crucible of technical expertise in building dikes and embankments. By the 11th century, dike construction was proceeding hand in hand with the development of 'polders' and the reclamation of heaths and bogs.

Still the sea ate into the mainland. It enlarged the former Lake Flevo at the mouth of the Rhine into the Zuider Zee and washed away whole river marshes. The Dutch then began using wind-mills to pump out excess water so that, at high storm tides, rivers unable to drain into the sea did not flood the land. Between 1927 and 1932, a 30 km embankment was built across the mouth of the Zuider Zee, turning it into a freshwater lake, the Ijsselmeer.

I am thunder, I am lightning, restless mercury, never still,
Self-respecting, self-appraising,
bending others to my will.
And the sword which cut the gullet
of the tyrant was my own,
And the spark which burnt his wheat-stock
is from me and me alone.
The rich and wealthy hear my cry and thrust
their fingers in their ears.
Bring the axe and I shall swim the bloody river
of their tears.

Revolutionary, Makhdum Muhiuddin, (Pakistan)
translated from Urdu by David Matthews

Water to power machines

The idea of using the natural force of water to drive machines also dates back into antiquity. One of the earliest and most ingenious of contraptions was the bucket wheel, which was caused to rotate by the river's flow and could lift water to a height of 30 m/98 ft. This was used along the Nile, in Mesopotamia, and in China where it was constructed of bamboo. Water's power was thus first used to lift or haul water itself, into irrigation channels.

The use of water-power for driving millstones and making flour out of grain was introduced by the Romans. They brought water-mills to Britain, where by the time of the Domesday survey (1086), their creaking rotations were heard throughout the country: the Domesday Book mentions 500 in the counties of Norfolk and Suffolk alone.

Water continued to be the most important source of power right up until the arrival of the internal combustion engine. Steam – which drove ships, pumping stations, locomotives, agricultural and industrial machines of all descriptions – initially powered the industrial revolution, and the profound social and economic upheaval with which it is synonymous. Steam engines have been a source of inspiration to engineers, railroad magnates, hobos, children and romantics.

The age of steam is long since past, but water-power still has a role to play. Today, hydro-electricity – the use of falling water to drive massive turbine engines and create electricity – is still a major source of power, one claiming to be cleaner and more eco-friendly than alternatives such as burning fossil fuels or nuclear energy.

It was a steam engine, and I wished I had a camera to take its picture. It was a kind of demented samovar on wheels, with iron patches on its boiler and leaking pipes on its underside and dribbling valves and metal elbows that shot jets of vapor sideways. It was fuelled by oil, so it did not belch black smoke, but it had bronchial trouble, respirating in chokes and gasps on grades and wheezing oddly down the slopes when it seemed out of control. The whole contraption creaked, and when it was traveling fast, which was seldom, it made such a racket of bumping couplings and rattling windows and groaning wood that I had the impression it was on the verge of bursting apart – just blowing into splinters and dropping there in one of the dry ravines.

The Old Patagonian Express, Paul Theroux, 1979 (Argentina)

India, central Punjab. Ox-powered irrigation

59 / Hydropower provides 19% of the world's electricity supply and is used in over 150 countries.

Great dams

India, Khoteswar, Narmada River. Temple submerged by the Sardar Sarovar Dam

Around 45,000 large dams (15 m in height, or with reservoirs of 3 million cu. m) have been constructed globally, displacing at least 80 million people.

The great dams, whose own era dawned in the early 20th century, are the principal generators of hydropower. South America is home to several monster hydrodams: the largest in the world is Itaipú on the Brazilian-Paraguayan border, with a generating capacity of 12,600 megawatts.

The increasing demand for electricity, as well as for irrigation and flood control, is the main justification for building these vast monuments to humanity's conquest of nature's forces. They belong to the technocratic ideology fostered by both capitalists and communists which centralized the management of environmental resources in corporate and state hands.

For many decades, dams were adulated as the epitome of progress. The new leaders of the developing world fell under their spell. In India, Jawaharlal Nehru (Prime Minister, 1947-64) was deeply enamored of dams and their potential.

As I walked round the dam site I thought that these days the biggest temple and mosque is the place where man works for the good of mankind. Which place can be greater than this?'

Prime Minister Jawaharlal Nehru, 1954

The dam-builders believed that they were bringing prosperity and progress. And in many ways, they were. But they were also very costly and environmentally damaging. And displaced populations showed increasing unwillingness to accept their removal – even extinction – as a justifiable sacrifice for the greater common good.

The Kedung Ombo dam in Indonesia displaced 25,000 people. Ghana's Akosombo, 80,000. On the Zambezi, the Cabora Bassa in Mozambique displaced 25,000, and the Kariba in Zambia, 50,000. Some 42,000 people had to move for the Itaipú dam (Brazil-Paraguay) and 72,000 for the Sobradinho in Brazil. The Sardar Sarovar on India's Narmada and its canal network, will displace 400,000.

Nowadays, no large dam can be built without vociferous protest. From Hungary, to Turkey, to the Philippines, to Paraguay, soldiers stand guard over construction sites and herd the dam-displaced to their new homes. The language of repression accompanies the modern exercise of hydraulic power against people who gain nothing from this form of 'development'. And sometimes lose everything – land, livelihood, health, dignity.

Before the submergence, we grew many things and grazed our cows in the forest. We ate well then – roti (bread), dal (lentils), curds, rice, vegetables, fruits, everything. Now look at our children, how thin they are. All we have now is the few rupees we make by selling firewood in the town. We can barely afford to eat – only the cheapest rice, boiled in lots of water. No pulse, no vegetables, maybe some forest leaves. Where is my husband? [Pause] My husband has gone to Jabalpur. He pulls a rickshaw there. We seldom see him. But at least I am sure that he is safe and he eats. What else can I say? There is nothing we can do.

Simi Lal, a tribal woman displaced by the Bargi dam, Madhya Pradesh (India)

Water at a price

England, Brighton. Billboard advertising privatized water

Two French transnational conglomerates, Vivendi and Suez, own or control water companies in 150 countries, and distribute water to 200 million people.

The power of water derives from its economic value – not just for agriculture, hydropower, and industrial activity – but for sustaining life itself. Water is a commodity, and can be bought and sold. Water-vendors, with their donkey-tankers and bucketfuls-for-sale, still ply their trade in some quarters of old towns, or out in dryland communities where public wells are few. As water becomes more scarce, many people can no longer collect it for free as they used to, but are forced to buy it from water entrepreneurs.

Today, water supplies have become increasingly engineered, running through pipes, pumps and taps, involving centralized civil engineering, treatment plants and the rest. Water first became costly to consumers in the Western world as a result of the industrial revolution and crowded living in towns and cities. The private water companies were expected to provide water and undertake a sanitary clean-up. But until water provision was taken into civic and public hands, and the price reduced, there was hardship.

I had occasion to go down a court where there are a number of cottages, but all without any supply of water. 'How do you get water?' said I to a widow, being in one of the houses. 'We steal it,' was her reply, 'and we run as far as we can for fear of being seen.' Yesterday, Elizabeth Stubbs appeared before the magistrates, charged with taking water from one of the taps supplied by the Preston Waterworks Company. The case being proved against her, she was ordered to pay a penalty and costs. An argument, thought I, in favor of cheap water.

From the local newspaper in the new industrial town of Preston, Lancashire, 1844 (UK)

... too high a price

Bangladesh, Dhaka
Selling bottled water

The idea that water is so precious that it cannot be treated as a 'free' resource and squandered thoughtlessly is sensible. Our lakes, streams and aquifers should be preserved for future generations. People with swimming pools and garden sprinklers should pay for their pleasures. But putting water supplies into private hands means that what comes out of the tap becomes a commodity on which profit is to be made.

International companies mop up lucrative contracts and make money out of citizens whose livelihoods are meager beyond belief, on something they cannot do without.

In the city of Cochabamba, Bolivia, the citizens said 'No!'

The guerra del agua (water war) began in earnest in February 2000. The people went to the central plaza to demonstrate against the contract with Aguas del Tunari (a subsidiary of the US Bechtel Corporation) and the high prices they were charging. Some occupied the plaza. Others set up a barricade across the highway. Women cooked for them. Many campesinos walked to Cochabamba to join in. Jubilados – retired factory workers – too.

On April 8th the government declared a state of siege. The plaza was filled with people. The Army fired tear gas into the narrow streets, and broke down barricades. Then a sharpshooter from behind military lines shot into the unarmed crowd. A 17-year-old student, Victor Hugo Daza, was killed. That was the end of Aguas del Tunari. Within days, the company fled.

Leasing the Rain, William Finnegan, 2002 (Bolivia)

Today, stories of hardship come from countries in the developing world, as water moves back from public hands to private. Public utilities are blamed for being incompetent and corrupt. Water leaks from their systems or is stolen, and failure to charge or collect rates means that they fall into disrepair.

But, for poorer people, the transfer to the private sector typically leads to distress. Mary Agyekum of Ghana, driven off her family farm by a mining company, now lives in a shanty-town and breaks stones for £2 ($3.20) a week. She and her family used to have free access to water. Now she has to buy it by the bucket. And pays a great deal more than those with taps and water closets living in leafy suburbia.

Russia, Norlisk. Holidaymakers beside a leaking sewage pipe

CHAPTER 4

Living and working on water

Malaysia, Sempurna. Stilt dwellings for illegal immigrants from the Philippines who cannot set foot on Malaysian soil

The stream is the village's life-line. It meanders from rock to rock, pool to pool, past wallows under the muddy banks in which buffaloes lie, their cool grey tonnage tucked into the curved recesses they have worn.

Playing with water
(Philippines)

Hong Kong. Houseboats in Causeway Bay

Water is decisive in where people live, whether they are nomads, farmers, fishing people, pastoralists or urban dwellers. All the world's great cities and towns sprang up around water sources. Some cities have had to be abandoned because they drank up their water and perished.

One such city is Fatehpur Sikri, south west of Agra, in India. Built between 1569 and 1585 by the great Mughul Emperor Akbar, it has lain silent for four centuries. But the years in Fatehpur Sikri were splendid. No comfort was spared.

Caravans with melons and grapes arrived almost all the year round from whatever district was now in its fruit season. A boatload of ice called daily at the capital in an unending convoy from the mountains between the Punjab and Kashmir. Akbar never drank anything but Ganges water, wherever he might be, but authorized the use of rainwater for cooking.

The Great Moghuls, Bamber Gascoigne, 1971 (India)

Water dictates rural settlement too. Bangladesh, the country with the most densely settled rural countryside in the world – 800 people per square kilometer – is among the wettest. Every year, the melting snows of the Himalayas descend through Nepal and India in the mighty Ganges and Brahmaputra rivers, flooding one-third or more of the country.

Thousands of villages become encircled by water. The flood brings the country extraordinary, even dazzling, fertility. But it is also inextricable from over-crowdedness, poverty and ill-health: too many people living on the margins of nature's bounty, too much pollution.

Many countries have similar water-bound environments, riverine and lakeside communities who make their living off fish and aquatic abundance, and who are more at home on water than on dry land. They are invariably among those whose lifestyle is simple – and fragile in today's world.

An Giang is a delta province. Through the fronds of the foliage, I see everywhere ditches, ponds, streams, canals, rivers and hundreds upon hundreds of boats. The Boat Country! Most of the dwellings seem to be surrounded by water. It is a land where you don't have to go to sea to catch fish. You just drop your line or a net over your front doorstep.

Romancing Vietnam, Justin Wintle, 1991

Burma, Inle Lake. Floating gardens

69 / Water determines population density. In the desert country of Niger, there are 21 people per sq mile; in watery Bangladesh, 2,401 per sq mile.

Desert places

Human settlement is at its most sparse where water is lacking. In desert areas, the distances that have to be traveled between water-holes, wells, oases and **wadis** (seasonal water courses) dictate a nomadic lifestyle.

For some peoples, like the San of Southern Africa, or the Australian aboriginals, life may be so mobile in the quest for food and water that no solid shelter is ever constructed. Others, like the Maasai of Kenya and Tanzania and the Herero of Namibia and Botswana, live off their herds and move to different grazing grounds with the season. These livelihoods, too, are fragile.

My father and his ancestors were pastoralists, so I consider myself one too. To be a pastoralist, one needs animals. To travel with these animals, donkeys are necessary – they carry women and luggage. To provide drinking water, one has always to carry outres. **These are goatskins filled with water which keep the water cool.**

We often arrived at wells with insufficient water to quench our animals' thirst, and the only thing to do was build another well. As a rule of thumb, we assumed a meter a day could be dug – though the deeper wells took longer. Before digging, the area was examined to find the most likely place. We dug with wood and iron tools, then the walls were lined with thin flexible strips of vegetation to prevent sand falling into the well.

At the desert's edge, Hadi Ould Saleck, who lost his herds to drought in the 1980s (Mauritania)

Yet others in Northern Africa, the Middle East and Central Asia depend on their camels. This is the 'ship of the desert', whose long eyelashes, splayed feet, and need to drink only at many days' interval are attuned to sun, heat and sand.

Those who live off their camel herds are among the toughest and most independent-minded people in the world. Their camels matter to them above everything: they are bank, transport, food store, and make life possible where otherwise no-one could survive.

In the plains of Gardo and Galcaio where the scarcity of water is unbelievable, only hardy camels can survive. The Somali herdsman love their camels above all – even above their wives. They are valued not only because of their resistance to thirst – they drink only 30-35 liters of water once a month! – but for their astonishing frugality and ruggedness. During the long periods of drought they are content to eat the twigs of the stunted scrub, so tough and thorny as to make their lips bleed.

Their greatest gift of all is to supply the herdsmen with their entire diet. When the weather is not too dry and grazing abundant, each person drinks 8-10 liters of camel's milk a day.

Watering the camels at the rivers is an orderly affair even when there are hundreds of them. But it is not so simple at the wells as the animals tend to stampede. The exhausting work of drawing up water from great depths – in a leaky bucket made from a camel's stomach – increases the likelihood of the herdsmen quarrelling and fighting.

Lights of Somalia, Francesca R. Lapiccirella, 1960

Algeria, Doanet. Bottle break for the camel

71 /   Fully-loaded camels can travel 25 miles for 3 days across the desert, drinking only on the 4th day.

Fishing

China. Navotas fish market

Fishing is a form of hunting – the only ancient form of food gathering which still makes a very large contribution to our diet. In rivers, in lakes, in streams, around the coast, and far out in the ocean, people go off to catch fish. They use every conceivable device: spears, nets, baskets, traps, hooks, lines and trawls. Fish are baited with flies, worms, grubs, other small fish or lures.

Fishing people may sit patiently on the riverbank or shore. They may set off in canoes, as in Amazonia, carrying harpoons to spear huge pirarucu fish weighing up to 400 pounds (180 kg), as they bask oblivious to danger in lakeside shallows. Deep-water fishing is full of risk – only reduced, not eliminated, by modern forecasting and navigational aids. And ordinary fishing people everywhere face problems of competition from better-heeled operators.

Nigeria
Arbunca fishing festival

We set out across a broad lagoon scattered with Chinese fishing nets and floating human heads. When the heads, wagging agitatedly, began drifting out of our way I realized that they belonged to men walking across the shallow lake bottom; a few gave us glittering smiles as we chugged by.

The ticket collector said the bottom walkers were poor men who aspired, above all, to the wealth and status of a Chinese 'fish machine'. These, suspended above the water like huge surreal butterflies, spoke of better, easier, more spacious lives. Men had been known to kill for one, though marriage into a net-owning family was the usual way for those craving advancement. Set on a wooden platform, lowered and raised by an archaic Archimedean cantilever weighted with rocks, you simply lit a lamp to lure the shoals, dropped your net into the night tide and cranked it up again in the morning, full of money.

Chasing the Monsoon, Alexander Frater, 1994 (India)

Like primitive hunters, fishers tend to pursue their prey until an area is fished out, and then move on. Today, there are quarrels over hunting-grounds as different 'tribes' compete for dwindling stocks. There are serious disputes, sometimes erupting into violence, for fishermen – like other nomads – are notoriously tough. There were three 'cod wars' between Britain and Iceland in the 1970s. In 1994 Spanish and French boats came to blows in the Bay of Biscay. Fishermen have also been hurt in disputes between the Chinese and Taiwanese.

The sharing of fish stocks poses real strains on relations between communities large and small, powerful and weak as the limits to exhaustive fishing become apparent and corporate fishing fleets hoover up the catches.

More than 21 million people in the world make their living from fishing full-time, and 200 million depend to some extent on fishing for their livelihood.

India, Kerala. Known as **cheena vala** or Chinese nets, these elaborate structures were introduced by traders from the court of Kublai Khan

75 /   Between 1950 and 1990, the total world catch of fish increased fivefold. Over 70% of the world's fisheries are now fully or over-exploited.

Water carriage

For many centuries, rivers were more important than roads as thoroughfares and communications networks. Every city of major importance in Europe had flowing water at its hub, and on and around this water many jobs and occupations depended. Rivers could only be crossed by boat except where there were bridges, few of which existed until the 18th or 19th centuries.

River-boat was the principal, most convenient and pleasantest way of moving about town, and from town to the adjacent countryside – from London to Chelsea or Richmond, for example. In 1634, when Hackney Hell Carts and the new sedan chairs arrived in London, the 3,000 water-men who rowed for hire for a city population of 250,000 became worried about their livelihoods.

**Carroaches, coaches, jades and Flanders mares
Do rob us of our shares, our wares, our fares;
Against the ground we stand and knock our heels,
Whilst all our profit runs away on wheels.**
John Taylor, Water Poet and Royal Waterman, 1634 (UK)

In many parts of the world the open canoe was the standard means of traveling along rivers, and in the Pacific, from island to island. In some cases, skins or bark were tightly stretched over light wooden frames. In others, notably in Africa, Asia and the Pacific, a tree trunk – sometimes a very large one – would be dug out. These water vehicles served as passenger traffic, for moving goods, and even for fighting purposes. Some were large enough for long sea voyages.

In Zambia, a very special barge makes an annual outing to this day. The chief of the Lozi people, known as the Litunga, has for centuries occupied a dry season capital in Laelui in the flood plains of the Zambezi.

Every year, when the rains come, he must move all his goods and family to higher ground at Limulunga. This is an occasion for great ceremony. Drums sound, and the members of the royal court pack their goods in a flotilla of canoes for the six-hour journey. The fleet is headed by the Nalikwanda, the Litunga's barge, with 30 paddlers, all in fine array. A huge crowd greets his arrival, and dancing and singing continues all night.

The Nalikwanda is around ninety foot long and fifteen foot wide. She is made of planks held together with strips of iron; where the end of one plank is joined to the end of the next, these iron strips cross and re-cross, forming the pattern of the Union Jack. The barge is replete with awnings of calico, and surmounting the whole is a symbolic elephant. Made of blue calico stretched over a framework of wattles, he is about the size of a half-grown animal. His anatomy is slightly erratic. His ears, spade-shaped, are hinged to flap back-ward and forward with the wind in a most life-like manner. He has large tusks made of white calico over pointed sticks, and a long trunk with a little curl at the end. His tail resembles a dissipated paint brush. His belly is made of sacking, on which the initials of a well-known trading-firm (BTA) are very conspicuous but rather out of place. A seam in the calico, where his mouth should be, suggests a merry smile, as if he is fully aware of what is going on around him.
Secretary for Native Affairs to Queen Victoria, 17 August 1898, Northern Rhodesia (Zambia)

China, Yangtze River. Cargo boats from Chongqing

77 / The 1,700-mile Yangtze River is the principal navigable waterway of China. The 35,000 miles of water routes in its basin carry intensive cargo and passenger traffic.

... and water-borne trade

Within large continental areas far from the sea, trade frequently followed the course of river valleys. Some ancient routes extended over great distances – amber was taken in prehistoric times from the Baltic along water routes to the Mediterranean to be made into ornaments.

Every river poses different problems of navigation: rapids, shallows, cataracts or waterfalls, where boats may need to be dragged out of the water. Voloki is the Russian name for places where boats had to be towed overland. These were common in the upper reaches of the Volga at a time when the forests of northern Russia could only be traversed along the rivers.

In rivers that are fast-flowing, great skill was required to navigate through rapids. On the cataracts of the Nile, ten out of every hundred boats were wrecked – but the Nubian boatmen, who were great swimmers, usually survived. Tremendous effort had to be made by brute human force to pull boats upstream against strong currents. This was done by 'trackers'.

Though the junk was now apparently safe, for it breasted the smooth, swift water of the second sluice and was no longer being thrown from side to side, the heaviest work remained to be done. I turned to watch the trackers, for theirs was now the heavy work of making many tons of cypress go uphill on a fiercely resisting roadway of water.

It was a moving sight to see 350 human beings reduced to the level of work animals; yet thrilling too, to see the irresistible force of their cooperation, for the 350 cloth shoes of their each step up the slope were planted in the same moment, and the sad trackers' cries, 'Ayah!... Ayah!' were sung in a great unison choir of agony and joy, and the junk did move.

It moved, however, more and more slowly, as the last and hardest test of the trackers' labour began – heaving the junk over the head of the rapid, over the round, swift crest of the sluice. The bow of the junk seemed to dig into the water there. The rope grew taut. The great crowd of towing men hung for a long time unable to move.

Then suddenly from midstream, from the very centre of danger, came a lovely, clear, high-pitched line of song. It was Old Pebble. I saw him standing on the deck, himself leaning as if to pull, hurling a beautiful song at the crowd on the bank.

On the proper beat the trackers gave out a kind of growl, and moved their feet forward a few inches, and the bow of the junk dug deeper into the head of the sluice. They took a second, firmer step. And a third.

I had never heard Old Pebble sing such a melody. He was in a kind of ecstasy. His face shone in a grimace of hard work and happiness. This was his life's goal: this instant of work, this moment's line of song, this accord with his fellow men, this brief spurt of loyalty to the cranky, skinny, half-mad owner of the junk on which he had shipped, and above all this fleeting triumph over the Great River Yangtze.

At last the junk raised its head, shivered, and shot suddenly forward into the still water of the pond above the rapids.

A Single Pebble, John Hersey, 1914 (China)

Bangladesh. Shipwreck

79 / The world fleet of shipping is around 520 million gross tons; oil tankers comprise around 150 million gross tons.

Man-made waterways

Greece. Corinth Canal

Huge canal schemes take years to materialize. A canal through the Sudd in Sudan was started in 1904; the Jonglei, proposed in 1958 to compete the task, is yet to be built.

The construction of canals began in ancient times, in China, Egypt and Mesopotamia. The Romans joined in. These schemes belonged to the era when emperors commanded the waters and hydraulic works, and the vast slave workforces that made them possible.

King Necos began the construction of the canal to the Arabian gulf, a work afterwards completed by Darius the Persian. The length of the canal is four days' journey by boat, and its breadth sufficient to allow two triremes to be rowed abreast. The water is supplied from the Nile, runs past the Arabian town of Patamus, and then on to the Arabian gulf.

The construction of the canal in the time of King Necos cost the lives of 120,000 Egyptians. Necos did not complete the work but broke it off in deference to an oracle, which warned him that his labour was all for the advantage of the 'barbarian' – as the Egyptians call anyone who does not speak their language. He then turned his attention to war.

The Histories, Herodotus, c446 BC

Has anything much changed in nearly 2,500 years?

Early man-made waterways suffered from the defect that no-one knew how to transfer boats from one level to another, so they were practicable only along the flat. The Dutch and Italians both claim the invention of locks to move boats up and down elevations. In 1481, the Italian brothers Domenico of Viterbo constructed a lock-chamber enclosed by a pair of gates, and Leonardo da Vinci built six locks to unite the canals of Milan in 1487.

The Languedoc Canal (Canal du Midi) which joins the Bay of Biscay to the Mediterranean is the first modern canal in Europe. Designed by Baron Paul Riquet de Bonrepos, it was completed in 1681 – with 119 locks. This ushered in France's boom era in canal construction producing 3,000 miles of navigable water. In Britain, the Duke of Bridgewater led the way in 1759, with a canal from Manchester to his collieries at Worsley. Nearly 4,000 miles of canals were then constructed in Britain, before the advent of the railways.

The canals which, above all, captured engineering glory were the two great shipping canals, at Suez (completed in 1869) and Panama (1914). These, respectively, enabled large vessels to avoid circumventing the perilous Cape of Good Hope at the foot of Africa, and the dreaded Cape Horn at the tip of the Americas, both of which provided a graveyard for many noble ships.

Recent grandiose schemes on anything like a similar scale – such as the Jonglei Canal in Sudan to cut out a loop of the Nile, and a proposal for a Rhine-Rhône Canal – have fallen foul of international disagreement or popular protest.

The great canal, like the great dam, with all its overweening political might and its unforeseen environmental and social consequences, is destined to become a feature of an historic hydraulic past.

The water dependent

Chile. Fishing village at the edge of the Atacama Desert

Although the replacement of rivers and canals by roads as the primary means of travel, and the devouring behavior of the corporate fishing industry, have reduced the number of those directly dependent on water, nevertheless its influence over working and living continues. And livelihoods that have always been precarious and tough are becoming more difficult in a world where all those dependent on the natural resource base are being evicted to make way for those who commoditize water and the aquatic environment in order to make a profit.

The old proverb said: 'Give a man a fish, and you feed him for a day. Teach him how to fish and you feed him for life.' But in reality he – and she – knew how to fish already. Their real problem is that they are being forced out of the domain of fishing – and ferrying, and other water-work – into poverty.

In the past the old people would go to a sacred part of the reef where they would enact ceremonies and make sacrifices. The tuna would hear the messages and allow themselves to be caught. At the right time, the tuna would jump on to the end of bamboo fishing poles people used; the person would pull up the pole and the tuna would fly up and land straight in the canoe, as many fish as the villagers needed. At certain times the old people would not do the ceremony: when the fish had lots of eggs or when there were too many little fish. At these times, the elders respected the lives of the fish.

These days people still know how to call to the tuna, but the tuna are not happy to come. They look at the bamboo lines and say: 'Mi laes (I do not want to).' They see there is no respect any more. They have learned not to trust the hook.

Posala Unusu, Solomon Islands

Democratic Republic of Congo. Fishing on the River Congo

83 /   The EU has negotiated agreements with African nations for European corporations to fish their waters, paying around 10% of the value of the catch.

CHAPTER 5

Nourishing water

Ethiopia, Tississat. Fetching water from the Blue Nile River

The body of anything whatever that takes nourishment constantly dies and is constantly renewed. And if you do not supply nourishment equal to the nourishment which is gone, life will fail in vigor.

Leonardo da Vinci
(1452-1519)

Algeria, Gassi Touil. High-tech irrigation system

When we observe the crab in its mossy banks, we can only praise and admire it for all its art. For it is from the Heavens that it has received the power to nourish itself on oysters, a food so fine and so easy to obtain. Oysters are avid for water, and often install themselves among the rocks, their shells wide open, licking the mud. The crab seizes a stone on the beach between its tight claws. He sidles up furtively to the oyster, and thrusts the stone inside. Then, installed beside it, he feasts. The oyster, thus hospitable, remains gaping open until its death, while the ravisher eats its fill.

Oppian of Coryncus in Cilicia (Turkey),
during the reign of Emperor Marcus Aurelius (161-180 AD)

The most unpromising species, from beluga caviar to snails, cassava roots to bread-fruit, play their part in the nourishment of human life. Human beings and animals are willing to eat the most unappetizing foods in environments where water is scarce and hunger common.

Some nomadic peoples survive entirely on the milk and blood of their livestock. Many popular local foods – haggis in Scotland, grits in the US, **injara** (fermented bread) in Ethiopia, cabbage and pork in Eastern Europe, noodles in Vietnam, **posho** (pounded maize) in southern Africa – have evolved because they are easy to grow, cheap to process or buy, fill the stomach, and cover most nutritional needs.

The Chinese, a people constantly wracked by famine down the centuries, eat almost anything and are well-known for making the best of snakes, rats, and insects.

Namibia
Ovahimba mother and child

Nothing on earth can grow without water, whether plant, reptile, insect, crustacean or mammal. All living things contain large amounts of water in their tissues: in animals and humans, the proportion is 70 per cent. And within the vast cornucopia that nature has provided on earth, the survival of every species depends on its consumption of other natural things, whose capacity to fuel the lives of consumers higher up the food chain intrinsically depends on the water that allows them to flourish and reproduce.

Food and drink

Far back in time, ancient peoples discovered the art and industry of using soil and water so as to raise crops. The monumental records of Egypt provide the earliest information on farming. In the days of the Pharaohs, organized cultivation took place on great estates, using slaves or tenants as labor.

The crops were wheat, barley and millet, vegetables, herbs and roots. Ploughing and planting occurred after the annual flood, and some of the cultivation processes – hoeing and threshing – enlisted the hooves of sheep and oxen to press the soil and tread the grain. Winnowing was done by women. Such practices still continue in the developing world.

Wheat and rice are the world's two most important crops. In its native Asia, rice is not only the leading food, but virtually the only food for many millions of people. The monsoon climate, with its sudden floods followed by a long dry season, is ideally suited to rice cultivation.

The volume and pattern of water in the environment is one of the most influential factors in people's choice of staple food. Wheat and maize are usually rain-fed. Rice requires vast quantities of water, and is often irrigated. Some grains, such as millet and sorghum, are less thirsty than others and do well in semi-desert areas: sorghum yields much more nutrition for the same amount of water as rice, and many believe should be planted more widely.

A meal without rice is like a beautiful girl with only one eye.

Chinese saying

In the absence of water, millet goes into a dormant state; with the return of moisture it awakes with a start and begins growing excitedly, to take advantage of the water while it is still there. The Moors of the Sahara, great millet eaters, plant it wherever a rare heavy rain has temporarily filled hollows with water; it ripens 45 days after planting.

Food, Waverley Root, 1986

What people eat and drink, and how, are things of supreme cultural importance. Immigrants may retain their eating and drinking habits long after they adopt a new language. Most Japanese and Chinese do not feel that a meal is complete without a bowl of rice, regardless of how many other dishes have been served. In the Middle East, a meal without fresh bread is unthinkable, and if a piece is dropped on the floor, it must be picked up and kissed in atonement.

Most rural peoples brew beer or some form of fermented liquor from grain, vegetables or fruits. In many societies, beer may be preferred to water not only for its alcoholic and partying ingredients, but because it is less likely to be contaminated. On any local market day in northern Ethiopia, a small blue pennant outside a hut denotes a 'pub' or drinking place. The local plant used for brewing is **talla**, with dark green leaves and a strong bitter taste. Perhaps it came to be used for beer because it is fit for nothing else.

China, Shanghai. Food stall in the market

89 / For the same amount of water, sorghum provides 4.5 times more protein, more minerals, iron, and calcium, and can produce 3 times more food than rice.

Water scarcity, food scarcity

Bangladesh. Cattle feeding on water hyacinth

The freshwater crisis which the world now confronts is really a crisis about growing enough food in the future. Around 70 per cent of the water withdrawn from rivers, reservoirs and lakes is used for agriculture. To feed more people will require lots more water for irrigation. Where will it come from?

Although most of the world's cropland is still watered by the rain, the area under irrigation increased fivefold during the last century. Many of the world's sunniest and most fertile lands have been put under the plough. China, Indonesia, India, Israel, Japan, Pakistan and Peru all depend on irrigated land for more than half their home-grown food. But these systems are close to their limits.

Traditional irrigation works have been essential to food production since time began – witness the array of water harvesting systems in India, and the contoured and terraced **dambos** (valley meadowlands) whose waters are husbanded in Southern Africa. But many irrigation works have cost too much and had devastating environmental consequences. Waterlogging and salinization of the soil has curtailed plant growth and destroyed land, transforming it into glistening expanses of white sterility.

The most dramatic example is the Aral Sea, which has shrunk by 60 per cent since 1960. Each year, a huge toxic dust-and-salt cloud is lifted off its exposed shores and deposited on local cropland. The lake's ecology is ruined. But this is only one among many errors in environmental and economic planning.

Since 1951, 246 big surface irrigation projects have been initiated. Only 65 have been completed; 181 are still under construction. Perhaps we can safely say about projects started after 1970 that for 16 years we have poured money out. The people have got nothing back, no irrigation, no water, no increase in production, no help in their daily life.
Indian Prime Minister Rajiv Gandhi, 1986

There have been other unexpected consequences. Fish have been lost from rivers. Unwelcome species of aquatic plant have flourished. The water hyacinth is the world's worst water weed, doubling its mass in a few days. Its heavy leaves increase the rate of water evaporation, offer an ideal breeding ground for mosquitoes and parasites, clog waterways, sluices and channels.

A water hyacinth known as 'Kariba weed' invaded the vast lake behind the Kariba Dam on the Zambezi between Zimbabwe and Zambia. Before serious control began, Kariba weed covered 2,000 sq km of water with thick mats, some supporting shrubs and even small trees. The water below was starved of light and oxygen, killing fish and becoming 'dead' – undrinkable.

What was he doing, the great god Pan,
Down in the reeds by the river?
Spreading ruin and scattering bran,
Splashing and paddling with hoofs of a goat,
And breaking the golden lilies afloat
With the dragon-fly on the river.
A Musical Instrument, Elizabeth Barrett Browning (1806-1861)

To produce 1 kilo of wheat, 1,450 liters of water is required; for 1 kilo of rice, 3,450 liters, for 1 kilo of beef, 42,500 liters.

Where there is no tap

Bolivia, La Rinconada
Collecting ice

A supply of water at home, for drinking, washing and cooking, is vital to every household in the world. Where there is no tap, women are invariably the water-carriers. Millions of women still spend hours every day fetching water from the well, pump, or stand-pipe, carrying it home on their heads. Despite this, only recently has it become acceptable to ask village women where they would like a new source to be sited. In the past, men made all such decisions according to where it would suit them to construct the new well or standpipe, and on whose land.

In many rapidly growing towns and cities of the developing world, water is a scarce commodity especially in the poorer areas. It may be delivered by donkey or bicycle cart, and sold by the bucketful. Or, where there are stand-pipes, the supply may be regularly cut off for several hours a day. Disruption to water systems is also routine during wars and bombardments, enhancing the risk of epidemics.

Often, returning home, I found there was no water. The bombings broke the water pipes, and twice hit the Chungking electric plant. Most of Chungking anyway depended on the water-carriers, bringing water from the few mains or from the river 200 feet below us. Down, down, down and up, up, up, to get a pail of water ... and this yellow, turbid fluid, the sap of the Great River, cost five, ten dollars a pail. In bad periods I learnt to drink, cook, wash, clean, with only one pail of water a day.

Birdless Summer, Han Suyin, 1940 (China)

Water per head necessary for essentials: 21-36 liters. Drinking/cooking, 3-6 liters; washing, 15-20 liters (excludes toilets/baths); cleaning, 3-10 liters.

Pakistan, Peshawar. Refugee children taking water to their tents

The dark side of water

Ecuador, Guayaquil. Children swimming in sewage at Ila Trinitaria

Being able to wash hands with soap can reduce diarrheal infection by 35%.

Rivers and underground aquifers provide the world with its in-built cleansing system. The detritus we leave in the landscape, or jettison into pools and streams, is washed away by the rain and into rivers snaking their way towards the sea. But this means that rivers may contain hazardous pollution, and nurture organisms which threaten human life.

Thailand, Bangkok
Samutprakarn crocodile farm

I wandered by the riverside,
To gaze upon the view,
And watched the Alligator glide
After the dead Hindu,
Who stank and sank beneath the tide,
Then rose and stank anew.

And, from the margin of the tide,
I watched the twain that fled –
The Alligator, scaly-thighed,
Close pressed the flying dead,
Who gazed, with eyeballs opened wide,
Upward but nothing said.

Way Down the Ravi River, Rudyard Kipling, 1883 (India)

Many diseases are linked to contaminated water, or are contracted from an insect or parasite that breeds in or lives near water. In the long list of such ailments are included malaria, trachoma, bilharzia, guinea worm, typhoid, cholera, and all the diarrheas.

It is a man. He is poling a dugout across the river. The dugout is so deep in the river the man looks as if he is walking on water. He is standing with one leg forward and both hands on the pole, like a gondolier. His movements are measured and efficient. He is nearing the shore and we are behind him, closing in, when he vanishes into the reeds.

We enter the reeds where we last saw him, and at the end of a canal, follow his wet footprints ascending a bank, then along a passageway through the elephant grass. It penetrates deep into the bush, then empties into an enclosure. Five men are squatting on their haunches. They stand up and face us.

Using words in French and Malinke, we address the men. They stand dead still and say nothing. We point in different directions, but their heads do not turn. I look at the boatman, and make a gesture of eating. He does not respond, and I look into his face. Suddenly my eyes are jumping from face to face.

The pupils of each man are solid white. They have river blindness.

None moves. They are like wooden posts driven into the dirt, caryatids supporting the weight of the African sky.

A Journey Down the Niger, Mark Jenkins, 1997 (Mali)

Making water mean health

All societies know of the connection between cleanliness and health. This is why importance is attached to washing hands before and after eating, and other hygiene practices such as using different hands for eating and cleansing the body. The problem for poorer people is that water is so precious and such hard work to come by that bathing and washing are luxuries.

Among the better-off, protection from unclean-liness has often been observed to a point of obsession, especially in tropical climates.

Every day more than three hundred dishes were prepared for Motecuhzoma. Before eating, the Emperor chose whatever pleased him among the day's dishes: turkeys, pheasants, partridges, ducks, deer, wild boars, pigeons, rabbits. Then he sat down alone on an icpalli **(chair) and a low table was put in front of him, with a white table-cloth and white napkins. Four very handsome, very clean women gave him water for his hands in the deep finger-bowls called** xicales; **other plate-like vessels were held under his hands, and they gave him towels.**
Daily Life of the Aztecs, Jacques Soustelle, 1970 (Mexico)

Although there has been a push since the 1980s' 'Water Decade' to provide every household in the world with a reliable and safe water supply, the dream is still far from fulfilled. Under environmental pressures, the quality of water as well as the quantity tends to deteriorate. Millions of people in Bangladesh are at risk from arsenic in groundwater from naturally occurring lodes, which have leaked into the aquifers since the water table began to drop.

Other chemical contaminants also put human health at risk. Excessive fluoride in groundwater causes serious bodily debilitation.

In India alone, 62 million people are at risk from fluorosis, which can lead to skeletal deformation. In more 'modern' agricultural environments, pesticides and nitrogen fertilizers washed from the fields are also a threat to health.

The most risky pollutants of all are still the common bacteria which enter natural water courses because of all the raw human wastes deposited in the open in our overcrowded world. But in villages all over the world, good stories also abound.

For a long time the people were suffering. They drank from ponds infested with disease. And when the dry season exceeded its time, there was no water at all, not even dirty water. One year, 200 people from the villages in Okposi in Ohaozara died from cholera.

I started to make appeals. I went to the govern-ment headquarters in Owerri, and said that they should give us even an out-moded well, no matter how old-fashioned it was. They said that since long they had been coming and going to Ohaozara and trying all the possibilities, but that there was no water free from salt in all Ohaozara.

Nobody knew that one day such a team as Unicef would come. In October last year, they struck the first borehole bringing good water to the surprise of all. People who thought that they can only get water from a swamp now knew that water can come from a rock, and they were jubilating that Unicef has come to save them from the menace of cholera and guinea worm. Here in Ohaozara, the name of Unicef is now indelible.
Chief Awoke Obasi, Okposi in Ohaozara (Nigeria)

Nepal. Liquid and laughter on tap

CHAPTER 6   # Sacred water

Russia, Zagorsk. Father Gyerman brushes on holy water in an exorcism at St Sergius Monastery

For our well-being, let the goddesses be an aid to us, The waters be for us to drink. Let them cause well-being and health to flow over us.

The Ancient Rig Veda Hymn, **Water of Life**.

In many belief systems, water is held to have miraculous properties. Seven of India's greatest rivers are worshipped as holy. There are shrines and temples all along the banks, and pilgrims, barefoot and smeared in ashes, do penance and set tiny lamps bobbing on the water as an offering to their god.

In some African belief systems, life is a process of moving from being 'wet' to being dry. A baby is wet when born, and as the child grows up, he or she becomes 'drier'. An old and wizened person is clearly very dry. Among the Manyika of eastern Zimbabwe, children that die soon after birth are buried near the river. The oldest people are buried on the top of the hill.

India, Varanasi
Bather in the Ganges

In Cameroon, the Dowayo people despise fore-skins as causing a boy to be wet like a woman; a circumcised penis is dry and clean. When boys leave the village to be circumcised they have to kneel in the river for three days. When they are cut, it will rain continuously. Only when the dry season comes can they return to the village.

Rainchiefs are the high priests for the Dowayo people, holding the secret of life itself.

The rainchief showed me his portable rain kit. Once he had started the rainy season with the special stones on the mountain, he could cause localized downpours with the contents of a hollow goat's horn. He took me off into the bush, and we crouched down behind a rock. Inside was a plug of ram's wool. 'For clouds,' he explained. Then came an iron ring. This served to localize the effect of the rain: if, for example, he were at a skull festival, he would make it rain in the middle of the village until the people brought him beer.

Next came the most powerful part of all. This was a great secret that he had never shown anybody. He bent forward earnestly and tipped up the horn. Slowly, there rolled forth into his hand a child's blue marble. I questioned him about it. Was it not from the land of the white man? Certainly not; it had come from the ancestors many thousands of years ago. How did this stone make rain? You rubbed ram's grease on it.

The Innocent Anthropologist, Nigel Barley, 1983 (Cameroon)

Sharia, which in Islam means 'the way', originally meant 'the path to water'.

Mali. Celebrating at the Diafarabe Festival as cattle herds cross the Niger River

Assuaging the waters

India, Varanasi. A ritual bath in the Ganges

Water's supreme importance in people's lives means that, when it misbehaves, people have traditionally had recourse to priests and shamans to bring it back into line.

Among the great natural phenomena that the ancient Egyptians worshipped as cosmic gods – the sun, moon, sky, stars, seasons, eternity – the Nile was one. His name was Hapi, and as a sign of his fecundity, he had long pendulous breasts.

Water played a vital spiritual role, since it was the element through which the gods, and the dead, traveled on their eternal journeys. The sun-god Re sailed across the heavens in a ship called Manzet, 'the bark of the dawn'. At sunset he stepped aboard Mesenktet, 'the bark of the dusk', to be borne back from west to east during the night. Pharaohs were buried with elaborate boats, in which their spirits would venture across the celestial ocean, to become a star.

I have satisfied the God with that which he desires. I have given bread to the hungry, water to the thirsty, clothing to the naked and a ferry to him who had no boat.

Prayer inscribed on tomb walls in XVIIIth dynasty of the Egyptian Pharaohs, 1500 BC

Those whose livelihoods depend on the behavior of the sea or of unruly rivers treat the waters to which they entrust their lives with great respect. They persuade it to keep its temper by special hymns, prayers and rites.

O Holy Spirit, Who didst brood,
Upon the waters dark and rude,
And bid the angry tumult cease,
And give, for wild confusion, peace;
O hear us when we cry to Thee
For those in peril on the sea.

Hymns Ancient and Modern No. 370, M Whiting

The pilgrimage – **parikrama** – along the sacred Narmada river requires the pilgrim to walk both ways along the 1,300 km bank, barefoot, and eat only food offered in charity.

In the Tohono O'odham reservation in
Arizona, a shrine has been erected where
one day water emerged suddenly from the
open plain of the desert and swallowed four
villages. The people panicked and a council
was held among the shamans.

The first solution was to take a water-bird
to the gushing maw, and push it down. The
bird vanished, the water slowed a little – but
carried on: the people understood they had
been heard but not pardoned. Then a crane
was pushed in, with the same result. Then
a sea-turtle, and the water barely flinched.

The shamans then said two boys and two
girls should be sacrificed – an unheard of
act. People protested, but the water was so
threatening that finally they chose one boy
and one girl each from the Coyote people
and the Buzzard people. One grandmother
hid her boy by rolling him in a reed mat.

The four children, dressed in ceremonial
clothes, faces painted, were taken to the
roaring throat of water and forced inside.
When they sank from view, the flow ceased.
The water drained back to the earth and
a slab of rock was put there to seal the
children and water for ever.

When the grandmother returned and
unrolled the mat, her boy was not there.
There were just dry scabs of algae, as on
rocks when water drops down.

The Secret Knowledge of Water, Craig Childs, 2001 (USA)

Libya. Sand dunes threaten as the Sahara spreads

Tlaloc, the Aztec rain god, required the sacrifice of thousands of children to encourage the flow of their mothers' tears.

Cleansing water

The cleansing powers of holy water to wash away sin or confer spiritual purity plays a part in every religion. In the days of John the Baptist, new converts to Christianity were submerged in the River Jordan. Today, baptism is performed at a font by a priest, who says prayers, and makes the sign of the cross with holy water on the forehead.

Christianity is far from being the only religion in which water is used in naming and launching a new baby on life's journey. An Aztec midwife put sacred water drops on the new-born's tongue, saying: 'Take and receive this, for it is with this water that you will live upon earth, and grow and grow green again; it is by water that we have what we must have to live upon this earth.' Her incantation was to Quetzalcoatl, the feathered serpent-god of heaven and earth.

In Islam, the daily prayers are preceded by **wadu** – washing of the head, face, palms, arms (to the elbows) and the feet in a part of the mosque dedicated to this purpose. No-one may touch or read from the Qur'an without first carrying out **wadu**. At the Buddhist temple, the hands of the devotee must be washed before flowers are offered at the sacred places inside. The flowers themselves must be sprinkled with water too.

This process of washing, or ablution, also has a practical purpose: religions are precursors of public health. At Varanasi (Benares), the holiest city in India, thousands of people carrying small brass vessels descend the **ghats** – flights of steps and platforms leading down to the river – every day and bathe in the Ganges. The daily immersion, with its joyful swimming and splashing – and its prayers – is part of the rhythm of Indian life, starting as soon as the sun begins to rise.

Hindus always cremate their dead beside the banks of a sacred river – ideally the Ganges – if they can. If this is too difficult, their ashes are taken and sprinkled on the waters of a holy river.

O river, born of penance
Named by laughter,
Forests heavy with wild jasmine.
O holy Narmada.

Drop by transparent drop,
Each weighted with our separate sins,
You flow into the ocean's surging tides.
O holy Narmada.

You remove the stains of evil.
You release the wheel of suffering.
You lift the burdens of the world.
O holy Narmada.

The Song of the Narmada, Shankaracharya

Laos, Luang Prabang. A monk has a ritual wash in the Pi-May procession

'If the Child may well endure it, the Priest shall dip it in the Water discreetly and warily, saying: I baptize thee.' **The English Book of Common Prayer**, 1562.

Ceremonial water

Water plays a part in ceremonies conducted to make the great events of life auspicious. In Sri Lankan culture, water is an important symbol of fertility. Some of the rites performed at marriage ceremonies employ water in an attempt to ensure healthy procreation. One is called **ata paen vakkaranava**. The bride and bridegroom stand on a pedestal, and the little fingers of their right hands are tied together by a white thread. The father of the bride then pours water from a golden pitcher onto the thread, to make the couple's union fruitful.

In rural Botswana, when a bridegroom's relatives arrive to seek the bride, they come to ask for a 'calabash of water' – a poetic and symbolic expression for what is about to happen. This bride will be the water-bearer for her family. She will have been inducted into this task from the day she could walk unaided, helping her mother bring home water from the well from the moment she was able to carry a bucket.

How swiftly it dries,
The dew on the garlic-leaf,
The dew that dries so fast
Tomorrow will fall again.
But he whom we carry to the grave
Will never more return.

A Chinese burial song

Thailand, Chiang Mai. Throwing water at Buddha in Wat Pa Charoen Tham during the Songkran festival

In Sri Lanka, a person attending a funeral may be affected by **killa**, a pollution associated with the dead, and must wash or touch water on returning home.

Water, the avenger

Guatemala. Palms bow before the storm

In Russia and Siberia, ancient storm gods used the arc of the rainbow as a bow to fire thunderbolts at their enemies.

Water's supernatural powers, or the gods and goddesses personifying those powers, can be turned devastatingly on humankind. In Greek mythology, Poseidon – with trident in hand – could lash the sea into fury and split the rocks, causing fountains to emerge. But he had his kinder moments, and was also known as 'the preserver', since the sea was supposed to support the earth and keep it firmly in place.

Flood myths in which the order of the earth is temporarily destroyed by inundation occur in cultures in every part of the world. In Maori myth, the god Tawaki cracked the crystal floor of heaven and sent the waters of the sky cascading down.

In South America, the flood took place when the world tree was truncated, and the waters gushed up from subterranean wells through the severed stem. As in the story of Noah, two people free from sin invariably survive to rejuvenate a purified earth.

And the flood was forty days upon the earth; and the waters were increased greatly, and bare up the ark which went upon the face of the waters. And all the high hills that were under the whole heaven were covered. Fifteen cubits upward did the waters prevail; and the mountains were covered.

And all flesh died that moved upon the earth, both of fowl, and of cattle, and of beast, and of every creeping thing that creepeth upon the earth, and every man. All in whose nostrils was the breath of life, of all that was in the dry land, died. All were destroyed from the earth.

And Noah only remained alive, and they that were with him in the ark. And the waters prevailed upon the earth an hundred and fifty days.
The Bible, Genesis, Chapter 7

The guardian gods of certain rivers have similar powers. The Tonga people in Zambia believe that the spirit Nyaminyami looks after the Zambezi river as it flows through their territory. In the 1950s, the Gwembe Valley, part of their ancestral lands, was flooded as the waters rose behind the Kariba dam. The Tonga were miserably resettled on higher land, but their lives, hopes and livelihoods were destroyed.

Nyaminyami was angered by the removal of his people from the Valley, and during the dam's construction, he inflicted his revenge. On Christmas Eve 1955, the foundations of the constructional 'coffer' dam were washed away by a flood that swept down the gorge. Three years later, Nyaminyami caused another catastrophic flood; again the coffer dam was damaged. Although the dam was completed in 1959, Tonga people believe that Nyaminyami is biding his time and will one day cause an immense destruction to bring their valley back again.

The wind comes rushing from the sea,
the waves curling like mambas strike
the sand and recoiling hiss in rage
washing the Aladuras' feet pressing hard
on the sand and with eyes fixed hard
on what only hearts can see, they shouting
pray, the Aladuras pray. And still they pray,
with hands pressed against their hearts
and their white robes pressed against
their bodies by the wind.
One Night on Victoria Beach, Gabriel Okara (Nigeria)

CHAPTER 7

Water's delights

China, Shanghai. Weekend fun at the Dino Beach water park

How light we go,
how softly! Ah,
Were life but as
the gondola.

Dipsychus,
Arthur Hugh Clough
(1819-1861)

Delighting in water, carousing on water, playing with water: water is an element in which life is celebrated and enjoyed.

Water confers beauty on a landscape, with its sparkling fluidity, its crystalline reflections, its changing moods. The sight and sound of water is a source of spiritual refreshment: no grand building is without its ponds, streams and fountains.

Water is for sport and recreation too. Children splash in puddles, in paddling pools in the garden, and in sandy rivulets and rock pools on the beach. Swimmers breast the ripples. Surfers ride the waves. Lovers seek out watery bliss on the shores of the river, lake or sea, or steal softly over the lagoon beneath the light of the moon.

The Venetian gondola with its distinctive long, curving grace, its black elegance, and its gondolier – also the subject of poetic rapture – epitomizes romance. Today, gondolas ply the canals with their sight-seeing passengers, where once they provided essential city transport. This is the lot of many sculling and sailing craft – the Brixham trawler, the punt, the canoe – whose working antecedents were very different from their recreational role of today.

Being on the water has always carried risks. But even in the heyday of sail, of hazard from unforecast weather, and of frequent death by drowning, the risks did not put water-lovers off. Lord Byron, despite his withered leg, famously swam the Hellespont, a narrow seaway in the Turkish Dardanelles.

And I have loved thee, Ocean! And my joy
Of youthful sports was on thy breast to be
Borne, like thy bubbles, onward: from a boy
I wanton'd with thy breakers – they to me
Were a delight; and if the freshening sea
Made them a terror – 'twas a pleasing fear,
For I was as it were a child of thee,
And trusted to thy billows far and near,
And laid my hand upon they mane – as I do here.

Childe Harold's Pilgrimage, Lord Byron, 1814

Among the maritime peoples of the Pacific, swimming is learned by children at the time they learn to walk or even before.

Laos, Vientiane. Thanon Setthathirat, one of the capital's main streets

Water festivities

Many festivals are associated with water. Most derive originally – as do harvest festivals in the Christian tradition, or Thanksgiving in the US – from gratitude for the earth's fertility and whatever role unearthly powers have played in bringing forth its produce. People join together to salute the rains, celebrate the swelling of the waters, and applaud their vital contribution to prospects of health and wealth.

In Egypt, the festival of Amun, king of the gods, was held at the height of the Nile's flood (New Kingdom, 1540-1069 BC). Festivities lasted for 21 days, during which the sacred barges of Amun, Mut and Khonsu were released from their moorings and made their way to Luxor, escorted by a flotilla of boats and a huge procession along the banks. Many such festivals had a political purpose too. They showed rulers in their magnificence, impressed visiting potentates, and gave their subjects a holiday – and a good time.

In Sri Lanka, the Sinhalese people perform a spectacular ceremony after the harvest is gathered. This is known as the mutti-mangalle, the festival of the cooking pot (mutti), and is a tribute to the tank, or village reservoir, and the fertility it has brought.

Once a day has been appointed, an anumaetira:la – a person who represents a god and acts as his oracle – is invited. Everyone in the village contributes towards a huge feast, bringing rice, coconut oil, cakes and sweet plantains, as well as betel and areca nuts. When the meal is over, the anumaetira:la leads a procession, carrying two new earthen cooking-pots, incensed and daubed with saffron, and a betel nut offering, to a special platform set up in the shade of a tree, where they are placed. The anumaetira:la then sends up a powerful address to the god, and then, as the god possesses him, begins to dance. Dancing and drumming continue until dawn.

The god, through his oracle, informs the villagers that their offerings are accepted, and that their tank, their community, and all its inhabitants human and beast, are taken under his wing for one, two, or three years, according to the pleasure of his divine majesty. Then the people return to the village, bringing the anumaetira:la. He dances, and the drummers beat their tom-toms until the noon meal is served and eaten. After this, all disperse.

Water heritage of Sri Lanka, JB Disanayaka, 2000

Spain, Andalucia. Celebrating the crossing of the Quema River, part of the annual pilgrimage to El Rocio at Pentecost

117 /   Waters can bring fertility. In Greece in 4th century BC, girls bathed in the Scamander river before marrying saying: 'Scamander, accept my virginity.'

Enjoying the waters

Since time immemorial, baths have been places where water's delights are deployed both for cleanliness and pleasure. The Romans were the earliest architects of superlative public baths, with hot rooms and cold rooms, unguent rooms and vapor rooms, becoming ever grander and more luxurious with the expansion of their empire, and of the civil engineering feats which brought plentiful supplies of water into town. The Turks were not far behind.

Usually about once a week my grandmother had a sociable turn of mind and when these moods came upon her she invariably went to the Hamam. Hamams, Turkish Baths, were hot-beds of gossip and scandal-mongering, snobbery in its most inverted form and the excuse for every woman in the district to have a day out. Nobody ever dreamed of taking a bath in anything under seven or eight hours.

The young girls went to show off their pink-and-white bodies to the older women. Usually the mothers of eligible sons were in their minds for this purpose for these would, it was to be hoped, take the first opportunity of detailing to their sons the finer points of So-and-so's naked body. Marriages based on such hearsay quite frequently took place, but whether they were successful, few of us had any means of knowing.

In the hot rooms of the Hamams little jealousies and rivalries were fanned into strong fires and very often fights took place between the mothers of attractive daughters vying for the favours of the same young man.

Portrait of a Turkish Family, Irfan Orga, 1950

The city of Bath is one of many spa towns in Europe – Baden-Baden is another – which rose to prominence on the healing strength of its hot mineral springs. These gush from the earth at a steady 46.5°C. In the 19th century, 'taking the waters' was medicinally prescribed, and the whole industry of vacations and pleasure excursions to spas, watering-holes and the sea-side grew up around it.

Bathing is not a luxury only enjoyed by a few. In Bangladesh, where ponds and waterways fill the landscape, every person enjoys their daily bath, descending the steps into the tank, washing modestly so as to emerge clean and newly attired without revealing any intimate part of the anatomy. Children dive in and out of the water like fish, surfacing in ponds and streams with water jetting from their mouths. But this water is often polluted, so bathing in it – whatever the pleasure – may also be a risk.

If you would leave off your play and dive in the water, come, O come to my lake. Let your blue mantle lie on the shore; the blue water will cover you and hide you. The waves will stand a-tiptoe to kiss your neck and whisper in your ears. Come, O come to my lake, if you would dive in the water.

Rabindranath Tagore, Bengali poet (1861-1941)

Roman Emperors Agrippa, Nero, Titus, Caracalla, and Diocletian built monumental public baths called **thermae,** with swimming baths, warm baths, and baths of vapor.

Hungary, Budapest. The Széchenyi spa complex

Sport on the water

Many forms of sport on the water derive originally from activities with a much more serious purpose: ferrying passengers, naval contests, exploration and hunting for food.

Such a sport is fishing. The angler on the English bank or the fly-fisher in the Scottish stream may not primarily be trying to catch their supper. But once upon a time that was entirely what they were doing. Counterparts in many countries still are – although they, too, may take great pleasure in their sport.

He is an angler of the first force, this King of Britain [George V]. Behold him there, as he sits motionless under his umbrella patiently regarding his many coloured floats. How obstinately he contends with the elements. It is a summer day of Britain. That is to say it is a day of sleet, fog and tempest. But what would you? It is as they love it, those who follow the sport.

Presently, the King's float begins to descend. The King strikes. My God, how he strikes! The Hook is implanted in the very Bowels of the salmon. The King rises. He spurns aside his footstool. He strides strongly and swiftly towards the rear. In due time the salmon comes to approach himself to the bank. Aha! The King has cast aside his rod. He hurls himself flat on the ground on his victim. They splash and struggle in the icy water. Name of a dog! But it is a braw laddie! The Ghillie, a kind of outdoor domestic, administers the coup de grace with his pistol. The King cries with a shrill voice, 'Hip-Hip-hurrah!'

On these red letter days His Majesty George dines on a Haggis and a whisky grog. Like a true Scotsman he wears only a kilt.

Anonymous French newspaper reporter

Boating sports – sculling, rowing, sailing, canoeing – are enjoyed the world over. Dragon-boat team races – which today take place in Hong Kong, Singapore, Malaysia and are spreading elsewhere – originated in China. In 278 BC, the then state of Chu (northern Hunan) was under siege. The poet Qu Yuan, hearing of the imminent invasion, drowned himself in the Miluo river. Distraught locals jumped into their boats and raced to save him – in vain. They scattered **zongtzi** – packets of meat and rice wrapped in lotus leaves – into the river as an offering to his spirit.

Today's dragon-boat races – which in 1976 became an international sport – commemorate the rowers' hopeless rush. They are an entirely festive occasion, with huge quantities of **zongtzi** consumed, and keen competition between the boats of 10 or 18 paddlers, a steerer and a drummer perched in the stern with a vast, booming instrument to keep the rowers ploughing the water in unison.

Row, row, row your boat
Gently down the stream.
Merrily, merrily, merrily, merrily,
Life is but a dream.

Nursery rhyme (UK)

Water sports include: sailing, canoeing, kayaking, water-skiing, aqua-tubing, power boating, punting, rafting, rowing, sculling, scuba diving, snorkeling, surfing, swimming, diving, water polo.

Nigeria, Lagos. Regatta in the Lagoon

Peaceful water

Iraq, Baghdad. Fountains in Firdos Square

122 / Geneva, Switzerland, contains the world's tallest fountain: the **Jet d'eau**, a plume of water rising 145 meters at the edge of Lake Geneva.

Fountains were originally built to provide people with water for drinking and washing, and were great places for gossip and the exchange of news. But they were also often landmarks, designed to impress as well as refresh, ornamenting the beauty of flowing water.

The aesthetic pleasure of fountains, the calming effect of water on the senses and its healing for the troubled mind has led architects, urban planners and landscape sculptors in many celebrated directions. The cooling effect of water in formal gardens and courtyards has been routinely exploited in large buildings whose masonry is a heat-trap in scorching climates.

An example of builders who did magical things with water were the 12th-14th century Moorish rulers of Spain. The Lion Court in the Alhambra Palace, in Spain's Granada, is a superb example. A circle of 12 white marble lions watch over every nook and cranny of the court, holding on their backs an alabaster bowl, whose fountain plashes gently. Each lion spouts a fountain too, and the water collecting at their feet runs off into a cruciform of canals, leading via other pools and fountains to surrounding halls and pavilions.

What pleases me most in these new fountains is the variety of ways with which they guide, divide, turn, lead, break the water, and at one moment cause it to descend and at another time to rise. In these fountains, art is mixed with nature; thus they strive nowadays to assemble a fountain that appears to be made by nature, not by accident but with masterful art.

Claudio Tolomei, architect and philosopher, 1543 (Rome)

The Shalimar Gardens – one of the ultimate examples of pleasure gardens in the pre-modern world – were built on the north-east bank of the Dal Lake in Kashmir, by the Moghul Emperor Shah Jahangir. The Shalimar covered a rectangle 500 meters long by 200 meters wide and descended through five terraces. Most of the architecture has today fallen into ruin, but the water still frolics through this astounding layered garden.

At the summit, the viewer is captivated by a magnificent spectacle; with the lake and town at his feet, he glimpses beyond the verdant valley the unbroken chain of the Himalayas. The uppermost terrace of the gardens hugs the Mahadol, which is sacred to Shiva and crowns the vista with its lofty snow-covered peak. Hard by the precipice, a water pavilion encompasses a rushing mountain spring, and from here sends it down from terrace to terrace as a central canal. It flows over vari-colored tiles, now ascending in an upward jet, now tumbling downward as a waterfall, until, flanked by mighty, ancient avenues of trees, it reaches the lake.

A History of Garden Art, Mary-Louise Gothein, 1928 (India)

Today's pleasure gardens are, for the most part, public parks where people stroll, relax, meet up with friends, take their ease. Boating in many such parks is an integral feature of their pleasures – whether you are in Beijing, London, Mexico City, Stockholm or New York.

Water profligacy

The problem with water's delights is that, in our crowded world, there is a tendency to be wasteful with water, and to neglect the awkward matter of protecting freshwater sources – rivers, lakes – from pollution.

Apart from water used for baths, washing machines and flushing toilets, the extra use of water in modern homes is for non-essential purposes: car-washing, garden hoses, paddling pools, ornamental ponds. Golf courses, car washes and swimming pools are thirsty too: the more affluent the life-style the more water is needed to keep it afloat.

The remedy for growing urban profligacy with water will have to be higher charges for non-essential uses, and incentives to be much more efficient about spillages and leaks. Unfortunately, this scenario – in which water is no longer a natural and free resource but a commodity – favors the entry of commercial companies into 'owning' water, organizing water, charging people to go on it or in it, and discriminates against those who cannot afford to pay for these delights. And so the leisure use of water may price it beyond the reach of many for whom it is an essential common planetary resource.

This water is not only for me. It belongs to everyone – women, men, birds, animals, plants. It cannot be consumed greedily by one or a few.
Mahatma Gandhi (India)

Panama. Pool of a luxury apartment building overlooking downtown Panama

During a drought in Indonesia in 1994, residents' wells ran dry but Jakarta's golf courses received 1,000 cubic meters/1,308 cubic yards per course per day.

CHAPTER 8

Troubled water

United States, Michigan. Pollution by tailings from an iron mine

We are in a race with disaster. Either the world's water needs will be met, or the inevitable result will be mass starvation and mass poverty.

US President
Lyndon B Johnson, 1966

The world is running out of water. The statement is probably a little exaggerated, but that's what the doom-mongers say. And there is no doubt that the growing world population and its devouring thirst for water is putting our finite supplies under severe strain.

Large numbers of people are already suffering water stress – meaning that the available supply per head is less than 1,700 cubic meters per head. In Africa the figure is 300 million and growing, over one-third of the continent's population. In the Middle East, nine out of 14 countries face water scarcity – meaning that the supply is already down to less than 1,000 cubic meters annually per head. What happens when their populations double, as those of several will do within 25 years?

Whatever the global statistics on water scarcity – and they are prolific – the cubic meters and averages per head don't mean much in people terms. Especially as those who live in leafy suburbs and stay in fancy hotels, with messages in the bathroom to 'Save water please' and forego clean sheets and towels every single day, won't be the ones to suffer. The places where the lack of water is deeply felt is in water-short homes, villages and back streets.

In many parts of India – a country not yet on the official 'water stress' map – the dry season is a time of dread, of day-to-day struggle. In many villages in Tamil Nadu, for example, no-one gets more than 10 liters daily – less than a large bucketful – and on bad days, nothing at all.

It was a swift, silent raid, launched under cover of darkness as the train crept into Pudukkottai railway station in Tamil Nadu at 2.30 am. The passengers remained asleep. I was pinned back in the corridor with my knapsack. A befuddled security guard who had been dozing, leaning against his rifle, looked on helplessly as the men swarmed on board. They were armed with pots, buckets and jerry cans.

And all they wanted was water.

This they obtained by emptying the toilet tanks with practiced ease. A couple of minutes later, I was alone on the platform. They were gone. So was most of the train's water.

Everybody Loves a Good Drought, P Sainath, 1996 (India)

Sri Lanka, Hambatota. Waiting for a water truck or 'bowser' in this drought-prone region

Total annual freshwater withdrawals today are estimated at 3,800 cubic kms, twice as much as 50 years ago.

Driven out by drought

Burkina Faso, Beli River. Searching for the roots of waterlilies in the dried-up riverbed

Every year, lack of water spurs seasonal migration from countless villages in drought-prone parts of the world into better-off neighboring districts and towns to find any kind of work until their wells, fodder and crops come back to life.

Whole villages in parts of India may be more or less deserted for several months. It has become commonplace to move water about the country-side by train and tanker and tip it into wells to prevent people from having to move. Some even talk of moving water around by airplane in the future. On the high seas, the water super-tanker could soon become familiar.

Some villages in the developing world are turning the tables on water scarcity by a return to age-old techniques of water harvesting.

Communities along the Arvari river in the Alwar district of Rajasthan, India, used to be threatened with mass drought-driven exodus. Now they have built embankments and water traps all over their desiccated valley and transformed it into a verdant farming area. Their Water Parliament, in which 72 villages are represented, meets every black moon day (the day in the month before the new moon rises) and settles how to run their water affairs.

Those living in fragile deserts and on mountain-sides are most vulnerable to climatic and environmental changes wrought by pressure of people on the land, deforestation, soil erosion, and disruptions to river flows from dams and upstream pipelines. During the 1980s, a series of droughts in the Sahel, the semi-desert southern fringe of the Sahara Desert, caused great loss of livestock and permanent ecological damage.

We came to Wad el Hileau as refugees from Niger when we were young. There was thick thorn scrub with lions, elephants and monkeys here then. We settled by the Takeze River, which became our most valuable source of income. The river was clean and full of crocodiles and fish. People did not have to worry about gathering wood because the river was like a train or cargo truck transporting large trees and branches to our door – now it just brings dead bodies.

Fishing was a lucrative and easy business then: no government regulations restricted us. We fished all day in a small sumbuk **(wooden fishing-boat) and sold the fish in the market. Like all other commodities, it was cheap. The widened river has become yellow and muddy. Fish cannot live in mud and most have disappeared, so fishing has decreased by about 70%. Even crocodiles are rare, yet a few years ago, if you just touched the shore with your leg, hundreds would run towards you.**

At the Desert's Edge, Ahmed Salih, 1992 (Sudan)

Deserts are expanding. Every year 6 million hectares of productive land are lost, and 21 million more so impoverished that it is hard to grow crops or graze livestock on them.

Water conflicts

Mexico, Mexico City. Standing guard over a drinking-water pipe

Water is a sacred common heritage to be worshiped, preserved and shared collectively, sustainably used and equitably distributed.
Vandana Shiva, Indian environmental activist, 2002.

The pressures on water have led to growing competition between users – upstream versus downstream, agriculture versus municipal supplies, one state versus another over a river or underground water aquifer which pays no respect to boundaries. In some places these competitions are becoming truly bitter as the same or dwindling amount of water has to be split so many extra ways.

Most talk of actual water wars concerns the Middle East, where the flows in the Jordan, the Nile, the Tigris and Euphrates prompt endless inter-state wrangling. But there are threats in many other less well-known places. In 1997, for example, Namibia and Botswana nearly came to blows over the waters of the Okavango Delta. Desperately dry Namibia wanted to build a pipeline to take 20 million cubic meters a year from the Okavango. Botswana refused.

If the Okavango Delta is drained by pipelines, one of the world's most beautiful wildernesses will be lost, along with one of the last sanctuaries of the San (Bushmen); wildlife will migrate or die in vast profusion, and 100,000 people be pauperized, ending up in shanty-towns. On the other hand, what will parched Namibia do?

These dilemmas face literally millions of people and their increasingly worried leaders throughout the world today. Often, it is the remote habitats of tribal or aboriginal peoples who have least political and economic clout to defend their interests which are most at risk.

There runs a road by Merrow Down –
A grassy track today it is –
An hour out of Guildford Town
Above the river Wey it is.

Here, when they heard the horse-bells ring
The ancient Britons dressed and rode
To watch the dark Phoenicians bring
Their goods along the Western Road.

The Wey, that Taffy called Wagai,
Was more than six times bigger then;
And all the tribe of Tegumai
They cut a noble figure then!

Of all the tribe of Tegumai
Who cut that figure, none remain –
On Merrow Down the cuckoos cry –
The silence and the sun remain.

Just So Stories, Rudyard Kipling (1865-1936) (Britain)

Corporate water power

Not so long ago, it was taken for granted in Peru that the campesinos – Indians, needless to say – could only open their irrigation sluice gates to water their tiny holdings after the big estate had completed its own take-off from the canal. Laws had to be passed declaring that the large land-owners could not act as if they 'owned' the water but must share.

The battle between rich and poor over water has been underway for centuries. Landed proprietors – in India and South Africa for example – still have legal control over aquifers and rivers running through their land.

If access to water were to be governed by the law of scarcity, its price would skyrocket in such a way that the poor would not get a drop of it. Even if it seems wise to impose high water tariffs on industries, agribusiness and private over-consumers, poor people's access to free water must be guaranteed. Before any debate on the style of its pricing, water must be recognised as what it has always been: a commons.
Water is a Commons, Jean Robert (1994)

Today, the transnational corporations are asserting control over water and looking to garner huge profits from the world's fresh water crisis. In the name of cost-efficiency and conservation, governments are signing up to deals with private firms – local and international – which turn rivers into commodities and build installations which poorer people cannot afford to use.

A woman in a South African township, asked why she preferred to scrabble in the bottom of a dirty river bed to fill her water-pot rather than use the safe supply from a new local tap, replied that the cost of a bucketful would deprive her children of their evening meal.

Within a year of the privatization of water services in Buenos Aires (1993), the number of workers was reduced from 7,600 to 4,000 while the price of water rose by 13.5%.

China, Shenzhen. Cleaning windows at one of China's two Stock Exchanges

Corrupted water

Zambia. Irrigation from an underground spring

In Köln, a town of monks and bones,
And pavements fang'd with murderous stones,
And rags, and hags, and hideous wenches;
I counted two and seventy stenches –
All well-defined – and several stinks.
Ye nymphs, that reign o'er sewers and sinks,
The river Rhine, it is well-known,
Does wash your city of Cologne.
But tell me, Nymphs, what power divine
Shall henceforth wash the River Rhine?

In Cologne, Samuel Taylor Coleridge (1772-1834) (Germany)

Kenya, Nairobi
A helping hand across
a drainage ditch

Another pressure exerted on the planet's freshwater system is an overload of pollution. The industrialized life-style has inflicted on the world's waterways a burden of untreated sewage, pesticides, and industrial waste, endangering both the health of people and the health of the aquatic environment itself.

All over the world, urbanized and industrial life goes hand in hand with river tampering. 'Swamps' are drained, protective dikes are built, settlements colonize the 'new lands', and farmers plant whatever crops they like on the alluvial plains. This has happened everywhere: along the Yellow and Yangtze rivers in China, along the Missouri and Red in the US and Canada, among the fens of East Anglia, in Australia's Murray-Darling basin, and along the Rhine.

No-one realized to begin with that swamps were not just nasty places full of disease, but were integral to the river systems. Within 100 years, 80 per cent of the Rhine's alluvial basin had been cut off from the river.

When Germany began its economic boom after the second world war, unregulated industrial and sewage effluent poured into the river. Fish species began to disappear. By the late 1970s, biologists described the river as dead.

But this story has a happy ending. In 1991, an ecological master plan was set in motion, with the aim of restoring the Rhine's main stream to a healthy condition. Dozens of dams were removed from tributaries, wetlands were restored, and salmon fingerlings released to restore the adult salmon population. There is still nitrate pollution from wastewater treatment plants and fertilizer run-off, as well as metals – at declining levels – such as cadmium, lead, copper, and zinc. But there has been major progress. The Rhine has been brought back to life.

Niger, Sahara Desert. Every drop counts

I have lived in Ndedo village since I was born. The situation here was bleak. There was no water, and we had to dig pits to try and find some. Each year, the pits would dry up, and we had to dig deeper and deeper. It got very dangerous.

Once, two young children fell in and died. It was a tragedy for us all. There was also a time when eight people were crushed by rocks when the pit collapsed on them. One was my sister, Rapanja. She was only 30 and had four young children.

The water at the bottom of the pits was always filthy as there was cow dung everywhere. We knew it was bad but we had no choice. Every year there would be an outbreak of cholera. People would have diarrhea all over the place, including near the wells. I can't begin to count the number of deaths caused by these illnesses. Children died like goats, including three of my own.

When I heard we were going to get clean water I remember laughing, it was so funny to me. I felt like I'd had a huge burden lifted from me and that I was let out into the light from a dark tunnel.

I'm too old to crawl down those pits now to get water. Can you imagine what it was like? My legs used to shake with fear before climbing down those holes. Now, luckily, all I have to do is to turn on the tap!

Since we have had the new water source, life has really changed!

Nakwetikywa, a grandmother in Ndedo village.
Oasis, WaterAid (Tanzania)

A trickle of hope

Around the world, beavering away with modest pretensions, thousands of communities and local organizations are trying – often with outside support – to reverse their own water crises.

They may be crises of scarcity: extra boreholes, deeper wells, rainwater harvesting devices. Or they may be crises of health, to be solved by a safer supply, one without chemical pollution from arsenic or fluoride. People's movements are resisting large dams, seeking alternative, more eco- and people-friendly solutions for power and irrigation, and claiming fair resettlement for those to be displaced.

In Hitosa district of southern Ethiopia, local village water committees spent three years building 140 kilometers of pipeline, connecting 28 villages and three small towns to a water supply fed by gravity from mountain springs. Hitosa suffers from severe water shortage, so people's motivation was high. Today, the scheme – prominently supported by WaterAid – serves close to 60,000 people. The key to success was people's involvement, not only for digging trenches at the construction stage, but in paying for and running the services, and seeing to minor repairs.

In many other corners of Africa, Asia and Latin America, people are rejoicing at the solution of their water worries. It is these stories of hope that we need to hold onto, not the vast and numbing statistics pored over by conference delegations whose members have never set foot in villages off the beaten track.

While the international experts meet and discuss the world water crisis, countless inhabitants of the world's most water-troubled places are quietly solving their problems. Of all things to celebrate about water, their efforts and those of the people who work with them to make their dreams come true are the most heart-warming of all.

Travelling in late March with President KR Narayanan – who was scheduled to give a special award to village Bhaonta-Kolyala – in a helicopter to the Arvari watershed, we could see nothing but barren fields all the way from Delhi to Alwar. But suddenly we came across green and golden fields and realised that we had reached the oasis of the Arvari watershed. Nobody needed to emphasize the importance of rainwater harvesting any more. The President of India saw a more or less dead Arvari river, unable to withstand the burden of two years' drought, but wells were still full of water and, therefore, fields were rich and productive.

Anil Agarwal (India), 2001

Between 1990 and 2000, the number of those in the world without a safe water supply dropped from 1,126 to 1,099 million; coverage rose from 79% to 82%.

Pakistan, Baluchistan. Water as a toy in the Chiltan Mountains

Nigeria. Tropical downpour

I think it rains
That tongues may loosen from the parch
Uncleave roof-tops of the mouth, hang
Heavy with knowledge.

I saw it raise
The sudden cloud, from ashes. Settling
They joined in a ring of grey; within
The circling spirit.

O it must rain
These closures on the mind, binding us
In strange despairs, teaching
Purity of sadness.

And how it beats
Skeined transparencies on wings
Of our desires, searing dark longings
In cruel baptism

Rain-reeds, practised in
The grace of yielding, yet unbending
From afar, this, your conjugation with my earth
Bares crouching rocks.

Wole Soyinka (Nigeria)

I am the Alpha and the Omega, the beginning and the end. To the thirsty I will give water without price from the fountain of the water of life.
The Bible, Revelation 21:6

Bibliography

Names in square brackets below relate to the quotes/extracts found in this book's text.

Chapter 1

Philip Ball, **H₂O: A Biography of Water**, Weidenfeld & Nicolson, 1999 [Paracelsus].

Idries Shah, **Learning How To Learn**, Octagon Press, 1983 [Saadi of Shiraz].

Abdul Rahim Khankhana was a revered sage at the court of the Mughul Emperor Akbar 1556-1605. His couplets taught the meaning of life.

Gita Mehta, **The River Sutra**, Minerva 1994 [Traditional Indian raga].

Hans Silvester, Marie-France Depuis-Tate, and Bernard Fischesser, Water: **A spectacular celebration of water's vital role in the life of our planet**, Thames & Hudson, 2001.

David Kinnersley, **Troubled Water**, Hilary Shipman, 1988.

Anil Agarwal, Sunita Narain Eds, **Dying Wisdom: Rise, fall, and potential of India's traditional water harvesting systems**, CSE India, 1997 [Plato].

Paul Brown, '1953 flood, 50 Years On', **The Guardian**, 25 January 2003.

The Poetry of Robert Frost, 1874-1963, Holt, Rinehart and Winston, 1979.

Chapter 2

Lao Tze, **Tao Te Ching** verse 78; Lao Tze was a Chinese spiritual teacher of the 6th century BC.

Gretel Ehrlich, **This Cold Heaven: Seven Seasons in Greenland**, Fourth Estate/Harper Collins, 2002.

Eberhard Czaya, **Rivers of the World**, Cambridge University Press 1983 [David Livingstone].

H₂O: A Biography of Water, op. cit. [Paul Claudel].

Idries Shah, **Tales of the Dervishes**, Octagon Press, 1984 [Awad Afifi].

Marq de Villiers, **Water Wars: Is the world's water running out?** Weidenfeld and Nicolson, 1999.

Alexander Frater, **Chasing the Monsoon**, Penguin, 1991 [Joseph Hooker].

JB Disanayaka, **Water Heritage of Sri Lanka**, University of Colombo, 2000.

Chapter 3

Water Wars, op. cit. (King Solomon).

Colin Ward, **Reflected in Water: A Crisis in Social Responsibility**, Cassell 1997 [Karl Wittfogel].

Water Heritage of Sri Lanka, op. cit. [(King Prakrama Bahu].

John Hemming, **The Conquest of the Incas**, Penguin 1970.

Gerald Moore and Ulli Beier, Eds, **Modern Poetry from Africa**, Penguin 1963 [John Pepper Clark].

Madeleine Lynn, **Yangtze River: the wildest, wickedest river on earth: an anthology**, OUP, 1997 [Mao Zedong].

An Anthology of Urdu Poetry in English, translated by David Matthews [Muhiuddin].

Paul Theroux, **The Old Patagonian Express**, Hamish Hamilton, 1979.

Sunil Khilnani, **The Idea of India**, Penguin 1997 [Jawaharlal Nehru].

Maggie Black, 'Do or die: The people versus development in the Narmada Valley', The **New Internationalist** No 336, July 2001 [Simi Lal].

Reflected in Water, op. cit. [Lancashire newspaper 1844].

William Finnegan, 'Leasing the rain: Letter from Bolivia', **New Yorker**, April 8 2002.

Chapter 4

James Hamilton-Paterson, **Playing with Water**, Sceptre 1987.

Bamber Gascoigne, **The Great Moghuls**, Harper and Row, 1971.

Justin Wintle, **Romancing Vietnam: Inside the Boat Country**, 1991.

Nigel Cross and Rhiannon Barker, Eds., **At the Desert's Edge: Oral Histories from the Sahel**, Panos/SOS Sahel, 1992.

Francesca R. Lapiccirella, **Luci della Somalia (Lights of Somalia)**, Edizioni Lo Scaffale Roma, 1960.

Chasing the Monsoon, op. cit.

Works of John Taylor the Water Poet, The Spenser Society, 1869.

Ian Kazembe, **Discovering Zambia**, McGraw-Hill Singapore, 1972 (Secretary for Native Affairs 1898).

Judy Bonavia, **The Yangtze River and the Three Gorges**, Odyssey Travel Guides, Sixth Edition, 2002 [John Hersey, A Single Pebble].

Herodotus (485-425 BC), **The Histories**, translated by Aubrey de Sélincourt, Penguin, 1954.

Vicki Calgovas, 'The shark's children', in The **New Internationalist** 325, July 2000.

Chapter 5

Waverley Root, **Food: An authoritative and visual history and dictionary of the foods of the world**, Simon and Schuster, 1980 [Leonardo da Vinci, Oppian of Coryncus].

Modern Poetry from Africa, op. cit. [Jean-Joseph Rabéarivelo].

Patrick McCully, **Silenced Rivers: The ecology and politics of large dams**, Zed Books, 1996 [Rajiv Gandhi].

The Oxford Book of English Verse 1250-1900, Clarendon Press 1921 [Elizabeth Barrett Browning].

Jacques Soustelle, translated by Patrick O'Brian, **The Daily Life of the Aztecs**, Penguin, 1964.

Han Suyin, **Birdless Summer**, Cape, 1968.

Rudyard Kipling, **Echoes**, 1884 [Way down the Ravi River].

Mark Jenkins, **A Journey down the Niger**, Robert Hale, 1997.

Maggie Black, **Can Water Mean Health?** UNICEF News, 1980 [Chief Awoke Obasi].

Chapter 6

Nigel Barley, **The Innocent Anthropologist**, Penguin 1983.

Craig Childs, **The Secret Knowledge of Water**, Little Brown, 2001.

Pierre Montet, **Eternal Egypt**, translated by Doreen Weightman, Weidenfeld and Nicholson, 1964 [Declaration of virtue from the Book of the Dead, 1500 BC approx].

Yangtze River op. cit. [River Rites].

The River Sutra op. cit. [The song of the Narmada].

Water in Southern Africa, SADC/IUCN/SARDC, Maseru/Harare, 1996 [Nyaminyami].

Arthur Waley, **Chinese Poems**, Unwin Books, 1946 [Chinese Burial Song].

Modern Poetry from Africa, op. cit. [Gabriel Okara].

Chapter 7

The Poems of Arthur Hugh Clough, OUP, 1968.
The Poetical Works of Lord Byron, John Murray, 1905.

JB Disanayaka, **Water Heritage of Sri Lanka**, op. cit.

Irfan Orga, **Portrait of a Turkish Family**, Eland, London, 1988.

Rabindranath Tagore, **Collected Poems and Plays**, Macmillan New York, 1965.

Jeremy Paxman, Ed., **Fish, Fishing and the Meaning of Life**, Michael Joseph, 1994 [French Newspaper report].

Marilyn Symmes, Ed., **Fountains: Splash and Spectacle**, Thames and Hudson, 1998 [Claudio Tolomei].

EE Pfannschmidt, **Fountains and Springs**, Harrap 1988 [Gardens of India].

Chapter 8

Vandana Shiva, **Water Wars**, Pluto Press, 2002 [President Johnson].

P. Sainath, **Everybody Loves a Good Drought: Stories from India's Poorest Districts**, Penguin India, 1996.

Anil Agarwal, 'Drought? Try Capturing the Rain', CSE Occasional Paper, New Delhi, 2001.

At the Desert's Edge op. cit. [Ahmed Salih].

Rudyard Kipling, **Just So Stories**, Macmillan 1902.

Orin Starn, Carlos Iván Degregori, Robin Kirk, Eds., **The Peru Reader**, Duke University Press, 1995.

Jean Robert, **Water is a Commons**, Habitat International Coalition, 1994.

Oasis, WaterAid Newsletter, Spring/Summer 2003, www.wateraid.org.uk

Modern Poetry from Africa op. cit. [Wole Soyinka].

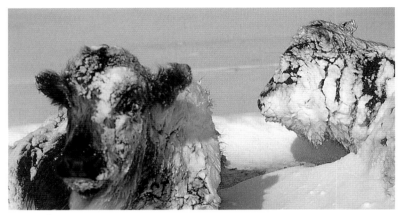

Photocredits

p. 1, UNEP, Still Pictures; p. 2/3, Clemens Emmler, Laif; p. 6/7, Christian Kaiser, Laif; p. 8, Frederic Denhez, Still Pictures; p. 9, Steve McCurry, Magnum; p. 10/11, Mitchell Rogers/ UNEP, Still Pictures; p. 12, Robert Frances, Hutchison Library; p. 13, Frans Lemmens; p. 15, Sean Sprague, Panos Pictures; p. 16, Ferdinando Scianna, Magnum; p. 17, Crispin Hughes, Panos Pictures; p. 19, Bruce Paton, Panos Pictures; p. 20, Jerry Callow, Panos Pictures; p. 21, J. Henderson, Hutchison Library; p. 23, Marco Paoluzzo; p. 24, Luchs und Progin; p. 26/27, Luchs und Progin; p. 28, Marco Paoluzzo; p.29, B&C Alexander; p. 30/31, L. Hong/UNEP, Still Pictures; p. 32, Trygve Bølstad, Panos Pictures; p. 33, Klaus Andrews, Still Pictures; p. 35, S. Rocha/UNEP, Still Pictures; p. 36/37, Martin Hawes, Still Pictures; p. 39, B&C Alexander; p. 40, ADI-UNEP, Still Pictures; p. 42, Mike Goldwater, Lookat; p. 43, Ian Berry, Magnum; p. 44, Frans Lemmens; p. 45, Luchs und Progin; p. 46, Georg Gerster, Network; p. 47, Steve McCurry, Magnum; p. 48/49, Julio Etchart, Still Pictures; p. 51, Chris de Bode/Hollandse Hoogte, Panos Pictures; p. 52, Nikolai Ignatiev, Lookat; p. 55, Mike Goldwater, Network; p. 56, Mike Goldwater, Lookat; p. 59, Daniel O'Leary, Panos Pictures; p. 60, Karen Robinson, Panos Pictures; p. 62/63, Hutchison Library; p. 64, Fred Hoogervorst, Panos Pictures; p. 65, M. Shteinbock/UNEP, Still Pictures; p. 66/67, GeenLim Eng/UNEP, Still Pictures; p. 68, J. G. Fuller, Hutchison Library; p. 69, Marco Paoluzzo; p. 71, Frans Lemmens; p. 72, Mike Goldwater, Lookat; p. 73, Hutchison Picture Library; p. 74/75, Jeremy Horner, Panos Pictures; p. 77, Chris de Bode/ Hollandse Hoogte, Panos Pictures; p. 79, Reporters, Laif; p. 80, Mike Schroder, Still Pictures; p. 82, Peter Gebhard, Laif; p. 83, Luchs und Progin; p. 84/85, Marco Paoluzzo; p. 86, Marco Paoluzzo; p. 87, Luchs und Progin; p. 89, Stuart Franklin, Magnum; p. 90, Fred Hoogervorst, Panos Pictures; p. 92, Eric Lawrie, Hutchison Library; p. 93, Paul Hahn, Laif; p. 94, Jeremy Horner, Hutchison Library; p. 95, Marco Paoluzzo; p. 97, Paul Hahn, Laif; p. 89/99, Nikolai Ignatiev, Network; p. 100, Paul Smith, Panos Pictures; p. 101, Rhodri Jones, Panos Pictures; p. 102, Raffaele Celentano, Laif; p. 104/105, Voltchev/ UNEP, Still Pictures; p. 107, Chris Sattlberger, Panos Pictures; p. 108/109, Mike Goldwater, Network; p. 110, John Fuller, Hutchison Library; p. 112/113, Fritz Hoffmann, Lookat; p. 115, Marco Paoluzzo; p. 117, Jochem Wijnands; p. 119, Martin Parr, Magnum; p. 121, Bruno Barbey, Magnum; p. 122, Stuart Freedman, Lookat; p. 124/125, Stephen Ferry, Lookat; p. 126/127, Jim Wark, Still Pictures; p. 129, Andy Johnstone, Panos Pictures; p. 130, Georg Gerster, Network; p. 132, Heiko Meyer, Laif; p. 134/135, Chris Stowers, Panos Pictures; p. 136, Guy Mansfield, Panos Pictures; p. 137, Betty Press, Panos; p. 138/139, Luchs und Progin; p. 141, Olivia Heussler; p. 142, Anna Tully, Hutchison Library; p. 144, Harriet Logan, Lookat.

Photo: Mongolia. Snow-covered cows in Ovorkhangai province